Tampa Bay Rays 2021

A Baseball Companion

Edited by Steven Goldman and Bret Sayre

Baseball Prospectus

Craig Brown, Associate Editor
Robert Au, Harry Pavlidis and Amy Pircher, Statistics Editors

Copyright © 2021 by DIY Baseball, LLC.
All rights reserved

This book or any part thereof may not be reproduced or transmitted in any form or by any means, electronic or mechanical, including photocopying, recording, or by any information storage and retrieval system, without permission in writing from the publisher.

Limit of Liability/Disclaimer of Warranty: While the publisher and the author have used their best efforts in preparing this book, they make no representations or warranties with respect to the accuracy or completeness of the contents of this book and specifically disclaim any implied warranties of merchantability or fitness for a particular purpose. No warranty may be created or extended by sales representatives or written sales materials. The advice and strategies contained herein may not be suitable for your situation. You should consult with a professional where appropriate. Neither the publisher nor the author shall be liable for any loss of profit or any other commercial damages, including but not limited to special, incidental, consequential, or other damages.

Library of Congress Cataloging-in-Publication Data:
paperback
ISBN-13: 978-1-950716-77-7

Project Credits
Cover Design: Ginny Searle
Interior Design and Production: Amy Pircher, Robert Au
Layout: Amy Pircher, Robert Au

Baseball icon courtesy of Uberux, from https://www.shareicon.net/author/uberux

Ballpark diagram courtesy of Lou Spirito/THIRTY81 Project, https://thirty81project.com/

Manufactured in the United States of America
10 9 8 7 6 5 4 3 2 1

Table of Contents

Statistical Introduction v

Part 1: Team Analysis
Performance Graphs 3
2020 Team Performance 4
2021 Team Projections 5
Team Personnel 6
Tropicana Field Stats 7
Rays Team Analysis 9

Part 2: Player Analysis
Rays Player Analysis 16
Rays Prospects 89

Part 3: Featured Articles
Rays All-Time Top 10 Players 105
    by Matthew Trueblood

A Taxonomy of 2020 Abnormalities 111
    by Rob Mains

Tranches of WAR 117
    by Russell A. Carleton

Secondhand Sport 123
    by Patrick Dubuque

Steve Dalkowski Dreaming 127
    by Steven Goldman

A Reward For A Functioning Society 131
    by Cory Frontin and Craig Goldstein

Index of Names 135

Statistical Introduction

Sports are, fundamentally, a blend of athletic endeavor and storytelling. Baseball, like any other sport, tells its stories in so many ways: in the arc of a game from the stands or a season from the box scores, in photos, or even in numbers. At Baseball Prospectus, we understand that statistics don't replace observation or any of baseball's stories, but complement everything else that makes the game so much fun.

What stats help us with is with patterns and precision, variance and value. This book can help you learn things you may not see from watching a game or hundred, whether it's the path of a career over time or the breadth of the entire MLB. We'd also never ask you to choose between our numbers and the experience of viewing a game from the cheap seats or the comfort of your home; our publication combines running the numbers with observations and wisdom from some of the brightest minds we can find. But if you *do* want to learn more about the numbers beyond what's on the backs of player jerseys, let us help explain.

Offense

We've revised our methodology for determining batting value. Long-time readers of the book will notice that we've retired True Average in favor of a new metric: Deserved Runs Created Plus (DRC+). Developed by Jonathan Judge and our stats team, this statistic measures everything a player does at the plate–reaching base, hitting for power, making outs, and moving runners over–and puts it on a scale where 100 equals league-average performance. A DRC+ of 150 is terrific, a DRC+ of 100 is average and a DRC+ of 75 means you better be an excellent defender.

DRC+ also does a better job than any of our previous metrics in taking contextual factors into account. The model adjusts for how the park affects performance, but also for things like the talent of the opposing pitcher, value of different types of batted-ball events, league, temperature and other factors. It's able to describe a player's expected offensive contribution than any other statistic we've found over the years, and also does a better job of predicting future performance as well.

The other aspect of run-scoring is baserunning, which we quantify using Baserunning Runs. BRR not only records the value of stolen bases (or getting caught in the act), but also accounts for all the stuff that doesn't show up on the back of a baseball card: a runner's ability to go first to third on a single, or advance on a fly ball.

Defense

Where offensive value is *relatively* easy to identify and understand, defensive value is … not. Over the past dozen years, the sabermetric community has focused mostly on stats based on zone data: a real-live human person records the type of batted ball and estimated landing location, and models are created that give expected outs. From there, you can compare fielders' actual outs to those expected ones. Simple, right?

Unfortunately, zone data has two major issues. First, zone data is recorded by commercial data providers who keep the raw data private unless you pay for it. (All the statistics we build in this book and on our website use public data as inputs.) That hurts our ability to test assumptions or duplicate results. Second, over the years it has become apparent that there's quite a bit of "noise" in zone-based fielding analysis. Sometimes the conclusions drawn from zone data don't hold up to scrutiny, and sometimes the different data provided by different providers don't look anything alike, giving wildly different results. Sometimes the hard-working professional stringers or scorers might unknowingly inflict unconscious bias into the mix: for example good fielders will often be credited with more expected outs despite the data, and ballparks with high press boxes tend to score more line drives than ones with a lower press box.

Enter our Fielding Runs Above Average (FRAA). For most positions, FRAA is built from play-by-play data, which allows us to avoid the subjectivity found in many other fielding metrics. The idea is this: count how many fielding plays are made by a given player and compare that to expected plays for an average fielder at their position (based on pitcher ground ball tendencies and batter handedness). Then we adjust for park and base-out situations.

When it comes to catchers, our methodology is a little different thanks to the laundry list of responsibilities they're tasked with beyond just, well, catching and throwing the ball. By now you've probably heard about "framing" or the art of making umpires more likely to call balls outside the strike zone for strikes. To put this into one tidy number, we incorporate pitch tracking data (for the years it exists) and adjust for important factors like pitcher, umpire, batter and home-field advantage using a mixed-model approach. This grants us a number for how many strikes the catcher is personally adding to (or subtracting from) his pitchers' performance … which we then convert to runs added or lost using linear weights.

Framing is one of the biggest parts of determining catcher value, but we also take into account blocking balls from going past, whether a scorer deems it a passed ball or a wild pitch. We use a similar approach—one that really benefits from the pitch tracking data that tells us what ends up in the dirt and what doesn't. We also include a catcher's ability to prevent stolen bases and how well they field balls in play, and *finally* we come up with our FRAA for catchers.

Pitching

Both pitching and fielding make up the half of baseball that isn't run scoring: run prevention. Separating pitching from fielding is a tough task, and most recent pitching analysis has branched off from Voros McCracken's famous (and controversial) statement, "There is little if any difference among major-league pitchers in their ability to prevent hits on balls hit in the field of play." The research of the analytic community has validated this to some extent, and there are a host of "defense-independent" pitching measures that have been developed to try and extract the effect of the defense behind a hurler from the pitcher's work.

Our solution to this quandary is Deserved Run Average (DRA), our core pitching metric. DRA seeks to evaluate a pitcher's performance, much like earned run average (ERA), the tried-and-true pitching stat you've seen on every baseball broadcast or box score from the past century, but it's very different. To start, DRA takes an event-by-event look at what the pitchers does, and adjusts the value of that event based on different environmental factors like park, batter, catcher, umpire, base-out situation, run differential, inning, defense, home field advantage, pitcher role and temperature. That mixed model gives us a pitcher's expected contribution, similar to what we do for our DRC+ model for hitters and FRAA model for catchers. (Oh, and we also consider the pitcher's effect on basestealing and on balls getting past the catcher.)

DRA is set to the scale of runs allowed per nine innings (RA9) instead of ERA, which makes DRA's scale slightly higher than ERA's. Because of this, for ease of use, we're supplying DRA-, which is much easier for the reader to parse. As with DRC+, DRA- is an "index" stat, meaning instead of using some arbitrary and shifting number to denote what's "good," average is always 100. The reason that it uses a minus rather than a plus is because like ERA, a lower number is better. Therefore a 75 DRA- describes a performance 25 percent better than average, whereas a 150 DRA- means that either a pitcher is getting extremely lucky with their results, or getting ready to try a new pitch.

Since the last time you picked up an edition of this book, we've also made a few minor changes to DRA to make it better. Recent research into "tunneling"—the act of throwing consecutive pitches that appear similar from a batter's point of view until after the swing decision point–data has given us a new contextual factor to account for in DRA: plate distance. This refers to the distance between successive pitches as they approach the plate, and while it has a smaller effect than factors like velocity or whiff rate, it still can help explain pitcher strikeout rate in our model.

Recently Added Descriptive Statistics

Returning to our 2021 edition of the book are a few figures which recently appeared. These numbers may be a little bit more familiar to those of you who have spent some time investigating baseball statistics.

Fastball Percentage

Our fastball percentage (FA%) statistic measures how frequently a pitcher throws a pitch classified as a "fastball," measured as a percentage of overall pitches thrown. We qualify three types of fastballs:

1. The traditional four-seam fastball;
2. The two-seam fastball or sinker;
3. "Hard cutters," which are pitches that have the movement profile of a cut fastball and are used as the pitcher's primary offering or in place of a more traditional fastball.

For example, a pitcher with a FA% of 67 throws any combination of these three pitches about two-thirds of the time.

Whiff Rate

Everybody loves a swing and a miss, and whiff rate (Whiff%) measures how frequently pitchers induce a swinging strike. To calculate Whiff%, we add up all the pitches thrown that ended with a swinging strike, then divide that number by a pitcher's total pitches thrown. Most often, high whiff rates correlate with high strikeout rates (and overall effective pitcher performance).

Called Strike Probability

Called Strike Probability (CSP) is a number that represents the likelihood that all of a pitcher's pitches will be called a strike while controlling for location, pitcher and batter handedness, umpire and count. Here's how it works: on each pitch, our model determines how many times (out of 100) that a similar pitch was called for a strike given those factors mentioned above, and when normalized for each batter's strike zone. Then we average the CSP for all pitches thrown by a pitcher in a season, and that gives us the yearly CSP percentage you see in the stats boxes.

As you might imagine, pitchers with a higher CSP are more likely to work in the zone, where pitchers with a lower CSP are likely locating their pitches outside the normal strike zone, for better or for worse.

Projections

Many of you aren't turning to this book just for a look at what a player has done, but for a look at what a player is going to do: the PECOTA projections. PECOTA, initially developed by Nate Silver (who has moved on to greater fame as a political analyst), consists of three parts:

1. Major-league equivalencies, which use minor-league statistics to project how a player will perform in the major leagues;
2. Baseline forecasts, which use weighted averages and regression to the mean to estimate a player's current true talent level; and
3. Aging curves, which uses the career paths of comparable players to estimate how a player's statistics are likely to change over time.

With all those important things covered, let's take a look at what's in the book this year.

Team Prospectus

Most of this book is composed of team chapters, with one for each of the 30 major-league franchises. On the first page of each chapter, you'll see a box that contains some of the key statistics for each team as well as a very inviting stadium diagram.

We start with the team name, their unadjusted 2020 win-loss record, and their divisional ranking. Beneath that are a host of other team statistics. **Pythag** presents an adjusted 2020 winning percentage, calculated by taking runs scored per game (**RS/G**) and runs allowed per game (**RA/G**) for the team, and running them through a version of Bill James' Pythagorean formula that was refined and improved by David Smyth and Brandon Heipp. (The formula is called "Pythagenpat," which is equally fun to type and to say.)

Next up is **DRC+**, described earlier, to indicate the overall hitting ability of the team either above or below league-average. Run prevention on the pitching side is covered by **DRA** (also mentioned earlier) and another metric: Fielding Independent Pitching (**FIP**), which calculates another ERA-like statistic based on strikeouts, walks, and home runs recorded. Defensive Efficiency Rating (**DER**) tells us the percentage of balls in play turned into outs for the team, and is a quick fielding shorthand that rounds out run prevention.

After that, we have several measures related to roster composition, as opposed to on-field performance. **B-Age** and **P-Age** tell us the average age of a team's batters and pitchers, respectively. **Payroll** is the combined team payroll for all on-field players, and Doug Pappas' Marginal Dollars per Marginal Win (**M$/MW**) tells us how much money a team spent to earn production above replacement level.

Next to each of these stats, we've listed each team's MLB rank in that category from first to 30th. In this, first always indicates a positive outcome and 30th a negative outcome, except in the case of salary—first is highest.

After the franchise statistics, we share a few items about the team's home ballpark. There's the aforementioned diagram of the park's dimensions (including distances to the outfield wall), a graphic showing the height of the wall from the left-field pole to the right-field pole, and a table showing three-year park factors for the stadium. The park factors are displayed as indexes where 100 is average, 110 means that the park inflates the statistic in question by 10 percent, and 90 means that the park deflates the statistic in question by 10 percent.

On the second page of each team chapter, you'll find three graphs. The first is **Payroll History** and helps you see how the team's payroll has compared to the MLB and divisional average payrolls over time. Payroll figures are current as of January 1, 2021; with so many free agents still unsigned as of this writing, the final 2021 figure will likely be significantly different for many teams. (In the meantime, you can always find the most current data at Baseball Prospectus' Cot's Baseball Contracts page.)

The second graph is **Future Commitments** and helps you see the team's future outlays, if any.

The third graph is **Farm System Ranking** and displays how the Baseball Prospectus prospect team has ranked the organization's farm system since 2007.

After the graphs, we have a **Personnel** section that lists many of the important decision-makers and upper-level field and operations staff members for the franchise, as well as any former Baseball Prospectus staff members who are currently part of the organization. (In very rare circumstances, someone might be on both lists!)

Position Players

After all that information and a thoughtful bylined essay covering each team, we present our player comments. These are also bylined, but due to frequent franchise shifts during the offseason, our bylines are more a rough guide than a perfect accounting of who wrote what.

Each player is listed with the major-league team that employed him as of early January 2021. If a player changed teams after that point via free agency, trade, or any other method, you'll be able to find them in the chapter for their previous squad.

As an example, take a look at the player comment for Padres shortstop Fernando Tatis Jr.: the stat block that accompanies his written comment is at the top of this page. First we cover biographical information (age is as of June 30, 2021) before moving onto the stats themselves. Our statistic columns include standard identifying information like **YEAR**, **TEAM**, **LVL** (level of affiliated play) and **AGE** before getting into the numbers. Next, we provide raw, untranslated

Fernando Tatis Jr.   SS
Born: 01/02/99   Age: 22   Bats: R   Throws: R
Height: 6'3"   Weight: 217   Origin: International Free Agent, 2015

YEAR	TEAM	LVL	AGE	PA	R	2B	3B	HR	RBI	BB	K	SB	CS	AVG/OBP/SLG
2018	SA	AA	19	394	77	22	4	16	43	33	109	16	5	.286/.355/.507
2019	SD	MLB	20	372	61	13	6	22	53	30	110	16	6	.317/.379/.590
2020	SD	MLB	21	257	50	11	2	17	45	27	61	11	3	.277/.366/.571
2021 FS	SD	MLB	22	600	95	24	4	31	81	50	165	17	8	.263/.331/.499
2021 DC	SD	MLB	22	628	100	25	4	32	85	53	173	19	8	.263/.331/.499

Comparables: Darryl Strawberry, Bo Bichette, Ronald Acuña Jr.

YEAR	TEAM	LVL	AGE	PA	DRC+	BABIP	BRR	FRAA	WARP
2018	SA	AA	19	394	136	.370	3.0	SS(83): -1.9	2.4
2019	SD	MLB	20	372	118	.410	7.1	SS(83): 0.9	3.4
2020	SD	MLB	21	257	126	.306	0.7	SS(57): -5.5	0.9
2021 FS	SD	MLB	22	600	126	.318	1.7	SS -1	3.9
2021 DC	SD	MLB	22	628	126	.318	1.8	SS -1	4.0

numbers like you might find on the back of your dad's baseball cards: **PA** (plate appearances), **R** (runs), **2B** (doubles), **3B** (triples), **HR** (home runs), **RBI** (runs batted in), **BB** (walks), **K** (strikeouts), **SB** (stolen bases) and **CS** (caught stealing).

Following the basic stats is **Whiff%** (whiff rate), which denotes how often, when a batter swings, he fails to make contact with the ball. Another way to think of this number is an inverse of a hitter's contact rate.

Next, we have unadjusted "slash" statistics: **AVG** (batting average), **OBP** (on-base percentage) and **SLG** (slugging percentage). Following the slash line is **DRC+** (Deserved Runs Created Plus), which we described earlier as total offensive expected contribution compared to the league average.

BABIP (batting average on balls in play) tells us how often a ball in play fell for a hit, and can help us identify whether a batter may have been lucky or not … but note that high BABIPs also tend to follow the great hitters of our time, as well as speedy singles hitters who put the ball on the ground.

The next item is **BRR** (Baserunning Runs), which covers all of a player's baserunning accomplishments including (but not limited to) swiped bags and failed attempts. Next is **FRAA** (Fielding Runs Above Average), which also includes the number of games previously played at each position noted in parentheses. Multi-position players have only their two most frequent positions listed here, but their total FRAA number reflects all positions played.

Our last column here is **WARP** (Wins Above Replacement Player). WARP estimates the total value of a player, which means for hitters it takes into account hitting runs above average (calculated using the DRC+ model), BRR and FRAA. Then, it makes an adjustment for positions played and gives the player a credit for plate appearances based upon the difference between "replacement level"—which is derived from the quality of players added to a team's roster after the start of the season–and the league average.

The final line just below the stats box is **PECOTA** data, which is discussed further in a following section.

Catchers

Catchers are a special breed, and thus they have earned their own separate box which displays some of the defensive metrics that we've built just for them. As an example, let's check out Yasmani Grandal.

YEAR	TEAM	P. COUNT	FRM RUNS	BLK RUNS	THRW RUNS	TOT RUNS
2018	LAD	16816	15.7	0.8	0.1	16.5
2019	MIL	18740	19.4	1.8	-0.1	21.1
2020	CHW	4830	3.7	0.3	-0.2	3.8
2021	CHW	14430	16.7	-0.6	1.0	17.1
2021	CHW	14430	16.7	0.4	1.0	18.0

The **YEAR** and **TEAM** columns match what you'd find in the other stat box. **P. COUNT** indicates the number of pitches thrown while the catcher was behind the plate, including swinging strikes, fouls and balls in play. **FRM RUNS** is the total run value the catcher provided (or cost) his team by influencing the umpire to call strikes where other catchers did not. **BLK RUNS** expresses the total run value above or below average for the catcher's ability to prevent wild pitches and passed balls. **THRW RUNS** is calculated using a similar model as the previous two statistics, and it measures a catcher's ability to throw out basestealers but also to dissuade them from testing his arm in the first place. It takes into account factors like the pitcher (including his delivery and pickoff move) and baserunner (who could be as fast as Billy Hamilton or as slow as Yonder Alonso). **TOT RUNS** is the sum of all of the previous three statistics.

Pitchers

Let's give our pitchers a turn, using 2020 AL Cy Young winner Shane Bieber as our example. Take a look at his stat block: the first line and the **YEAR**, **TEAM**, **LVL** and **AGE** columns are the same as in the position player example earlier.

Here too, we have a series of columns that display raw, unadjusted statistics compiled by the pitcher over the course of a season: **W** (wins), **L** (losses), **SV** (saves), **G** (games pitched), **GS** (games started), **IP** (innings pitched), **H** (hits allowed) and **HR** (home runs allowed). Next we have two statistics that are rates: **BB/9** (walks per nine innings) and **K/9** (strikeouts per nine innings), before returning to the unadjusted K (strikeouts).

Next up is **GB%** (ground ball percentage), which is the percentage of all batted balls that were hit on the ground, including both outs and hits. Remember, this is based on observational data and subject to human error, so please approach this with a healthy dose of skepticism.

BABIP (batting average on balls in play) is calculated using the same methodology as it is for position players, but it often tells us more about a pitcher than it does a hitter. With pitchers, a high BABIP is often due to poor defense or bad luck, and can often be an indicator of potential rebound, and a low BABIP may be cause to expect performance regression. (A typical league-average BABIP is close to .290-.300.)

The metrics **WHIP** (walks plus hits per inning pitched) and **ERA** (earned run average) are old standbys: WHIP measures walks and hits allowed on a per-inning basis, while ERA measures earned runs on a nine-inning basis. Neither of these stats are translated or adjusted.

DRA- (Deserved Run Average) was described at length earlier, and measures how the pitcher "deserved" to perform compared to other pitchers. Please note that since we lack all the data points that would make for a "real" DRA for minor-league events, the DRA- displayed for minor league partial-seasons is based off of different data. (That data is a modified version of our cFIP metric, which you can find more information about on our website.)

Shane Bieber   RHP

Born: 05/31/95   Age: 26   Bats: R   Throws: R
Height: 6'3"   Weight: 200   Origin: Round 4, 2016 Draft (#122 overall)

YEAR	TEAM	LVL	AGE	W	L	SV	G	GS	IP	H	HR	BB/9	K/9	K	GB%	BABIP
2018	AKR	AA	23	3	0	0	5	5	31	26	1	0.3	8.7	30	47.3%	.278
2018	COL	AAA	23	3	1	0	8	8	48^2	30	3	1.1	8.7	47	52.0%	.227
2018	CLE	MLB	23	11	5	0	20	19	114^2	130	13	1.8	9.3	118	46.2%	.356
2019	CLE	MLB	24	15	8	0	34	33	214^1	186	31	1.7	10.9	259	44.4%	.298
2020	CLE	MLB	25	8	1	0	12	12	77^1	46	7	2.4	14.2	122	48.4%	.267
2021 FS	CLE	MLB	26	10	6	0	26	26	150	121	18	2.1	11.7	195	45.5%	.297
2021 DC	CLE	MLB	26	14	7	0	30	30	196.7	159	24	2.1	11.7	257	45.5%	.297

Comparables: Luis Severino, Danny Salazar, Joe Musgrove

YEAR	TEAM	LVL	AGE	WHIP	ERA	DRA-	WARP	MPH	FB%	WHF	CSP
2018	AKR	AA	23	0.87	1.16	61	0.9				
2018	COL	AAA	23	0.74	1.66	69	1.2				
2018	CLE	MLB	23	1.33	4.55	74	2.6	94.7	57.4%	26.2%	
2019	CLE	MLB	24	1.05	3.28	75	4.9	94.4	45.8%	30.8%	
2020	CLE	MLB	25	0.87	1.63	53	2.6	95.3	53.6%	40.7%	
2021 FS	CLE	MLB	26	1.04	2.44	64	4.4	94.7	50.0%	33.2%	44.2%
2021 DC	CLE	MLB	26	1.04	2.44	64	5.8	94.7	50.0%	33.2%	44.2%

Just like with hitters, **WARP** (Wins Above Replacement Player) is a total value metric that puts pitchers of all stripes on the same scale as position players. We use DRA as the primary input for our calculation of WARP. You might notice that relief pitchers (due to their limited innings) may have a lower WARP than you were expecting or than you might see in other WARP-like metrics. WARP does not take leverage into account, just the actions a pitcher performs and the expected value of those actions ... which ends up judging high-leverage relief pitchers differently than you might imagine given their prestige and market value.

MPH gives you the pitcher's 95th percentile velocity for the noted season, in order to give you an idea of what the *peak* fastball velocity a pitcher possesses. Since this comes from our pitch-tracking data, it is not publicly available for minor-league pitchers.

Finally, we display the three new pitching metrics we described earlier. **FB%** (fastball percentage) gives you the percentage of fastballs thrown out of all pitches. **WHF** (whiff rate) tells you the percentage of swinging strikes induced out of all pitches. **CSP** (called strike probability) expresses the likelihood of all pitches thrown to result in a called strike, after controlling for factors like handedness, umpire, pitch type, count and location.

PECOTA

All players have PECOTA projections for 2021, as well as a set of other numbers that describe the performance of comparable players according to PECOTA. All projections for 2021 are for the player at the date we went to press in early January and are projected into the league and park context as indicated by the team abbreviation. (Note that players at very low levels of the minors are too unpredictable to assess using these numbers.) All PECOTA projected statistics represent a player's projected major-league performance.

How we're doing that is a little different this season. There are really two different values that go into the final stat line that you see for PECOTA: How a player performs, and how much playing time he'll be given to perform it. In the past we've estimated playing time based on each team's roster and depth charts, and we'll continue to do that. These projections are denoted as **2021 DC**.

But in many cases, a player won't be projected for major-league playing time; most of the time this is because they aren't projected to be major-league players at all, but still developing as prospects. Or perhaps a player will provide Triple-A depth, only to have an opportunity open up because of injury. For these purposes, we're also supplying a second projection, labeled **2021 FS**, or full season. This is what we would project the player to provide in 600 plate appearances or 150 innings pitched.

Below the projections are the player's three highest-scoring comparable players as determined by PECOTA. All comparables represent a snapshot of how the listed player was performing at the same age as the current player, so if a

23-year-old pitcher is compared to Bartolo Colón, he's actually being compared to a 23-year-old Colón, not the version that pitched for the Rangers in 2018, nor to Colón's career as a whole.

A few points about pitcher projections. First, we aren't yet projecting peak velocity, so that column will be blank in the PECOTA lines. Second, projecting DRA is trickier than evaluating past performance, because it is unclear how deserving each pitcher will be of his anticipated outcomes. However, we know that another DRA-related statistic–contextual FIP or cFIP-estimates future run scoring very well. So for PECOTA, the projected DRA- figures you see are based on the past cFIPs generated by the pitcher and comparable players over time, along with the other factors described above.

If you're familiar with PECOTA, then you'll have noticed that the projection system often appears bullish on players coming off a bad year and bearish on players coming off a good year. (This is because the system weights several previous seasons, not just the most recent one.) In addition, we publish the 50th percentile projections for each player–which is smack in the middle of the range of projected production—which tends to mean PECOTA stat lines don't often have extreme results like 40 home runs or 250 strikeouts in a given season. In essence, PECOTA doesn't project very many extreme seasons.

Managers

After all those wonderful team chapters, we've got statistics for each big-league manager, all of whom are organized by alphabetical order. Here you'll find a block including an extraordinary amount of information collected from each manager's entire career. For more information on the acronyms and what they mean, please visit the Glossary at www.baseballprospectus.com.

There is one important metric that we'd like to call attention to, and you'll find it next to each manager's name: **wRM+** (weighted reliever management plus). Developed by Rob Arthur and Rian Watt, wRM+ investigates how good a manager is at using their best relievers during the moments of highest leverage, using both our proprietary DRA metric as well as Leverage Index. wRM+ is scaled to a league average of 100, and a wRM+ of 105 indicates that relievers were used approximately five percent "better" than average. On the other hand, a wRM+ of 95 would tell us the team used its relievers five percent "worse" than the average team.

While wRM+ does not have an extremely strong correlation with a manager, it is statistically significant; this means that a manager is not *entirely* responsible for a team's wRM+, but does have some effect on that number.

Part 1: Team Analysis

Performance Graphs

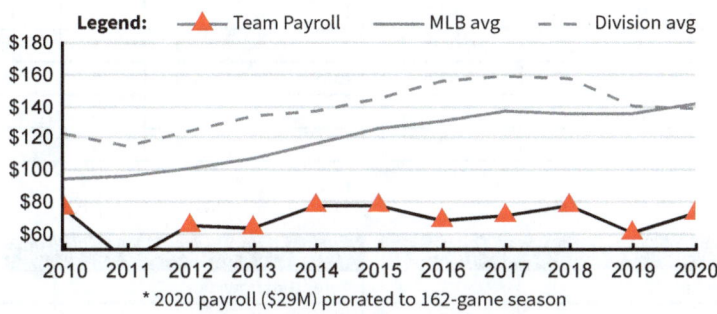

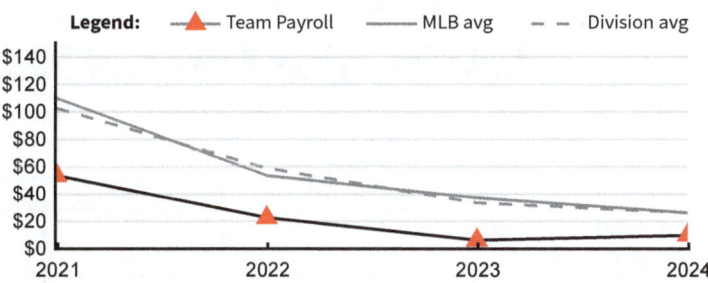

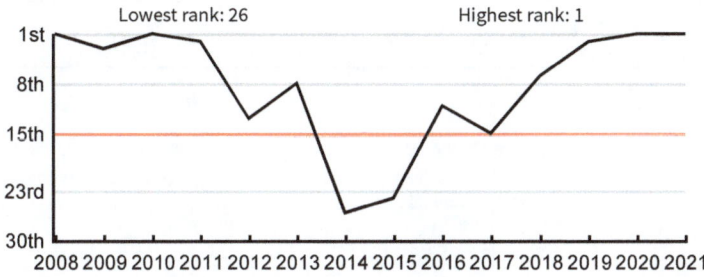

2020 Team Performance

ACTUAL STANDINGS

Team	W	L	Pct
TB	**40**	**20**	**0.667**
NYY	33	27	0.550
TOR	32	28	0.533
BAL	25	35	0.417
BOS	24	36	0.400

dWIN% STANDINGS

Team	W	L	Pct
NYY	33	27	0.560
TB	**29**	**31**	**0.495**
BOS	25	35	0.429
TOR	25	35	0.425
BAL	25	35	0.420

TOP HITTERS

Player	WARP
Brandon Lowe	1.2
Joey Wendle	0.7
Mike Brosseau	0.5

TOP PITCHERS

Player	WARP
Tyler Glasnow	1.4
Blake Snell	0.9
Charlie Morton	0.7

VITAL STATISTICS

Statistic Name	Value	Rank
Pythagenpat	.606	3rd
dWin%	.495	13th
Runs Scored per Game	4.82	12th
Runs Allowed per Game	3.82	4th
Deserved Runs Created Plus	94	21st
Deserved Run Average Minus	88	5th
Fielding Independent Pitching	4.03	7th
Defensive Efficiency Rating	.698	18th
Batter Age	27.6	7th
Pitcher Age	28.2	17th
Payroll	$29.0M	28th
Marginal $ per Marginal Win	$0.5M	1st

2021 Team Projections

PROJECTED STANDINGS

Team	W	L	Pct	+/-
NYY	99.5	62.5	0.614	10
The starting rotation was loaded with risk even before Corey Kluber and Jameson Taillon became members. At least D.J. LeMahieu should keep the lineup humming.				
TB	86.0	76.0	0.531	-22
The defending AL champions didn't really spend their winter defending anything.				
TOR	84.4	77.6	0.521	-2
They stopped a starting pitcher short of credibly claiming favorite status, but adding George Springer gives them one of the junior circuit's most lethal lineups.				
BOS	79.3	82.7	0.490	14
There's a faint flavor of their 2012-13 offseason to what Boston did this winter, and look how that year turned out.				
BAL	66.1	95.9	0.408	-1
Mike Elias was forthright about his disinterest in winning in the short term. His winter proved he was serious.				

TOP PROJECTED HITTERS

Player	WARP
Brandon Lowe	2.9
Randy Arozarena	2.8
Willy Adames	1.6

TOP PROJECTED PITCHERS

Player	WARP
Tyler Glasnow	3.2
Ryan Yarbrough	2.0
Nick Anderson	1.8

FARM SYSTEM REPORT

Top Prospect	Number of Top 101 Prospects
Wander Franco, #1	7

KEY DEDUCTIONS

Player	WARP
Blake Snell	3.6
Charlie Morton	2.2
Hunter Renfroe	1.7
Nate Lowe	1.0
Aaron Loup	0.5
José Alvarado	0.4
Aaron Slegers	0.3
Will Sherriff	0.3

KEY ADDITIONS

Player	WARP
Michael Wacha	1.5
Chris Archer	1.4
Francisco Mejía	0.7
Luis Patiño	0.3

Team Personnel

Senior Vice President, Baseball Operations/General Manager
Erik Neander

Vice President, Baseball Development
Peter Bendix

Vice President, Player Development and International Scouting
Carlos Rodriguez

Vice President, Business Operations and Analytics
Barry Newell

Manager
Kevin Cash

BP Alumni
Jason Cole

Tropicana Field Stats

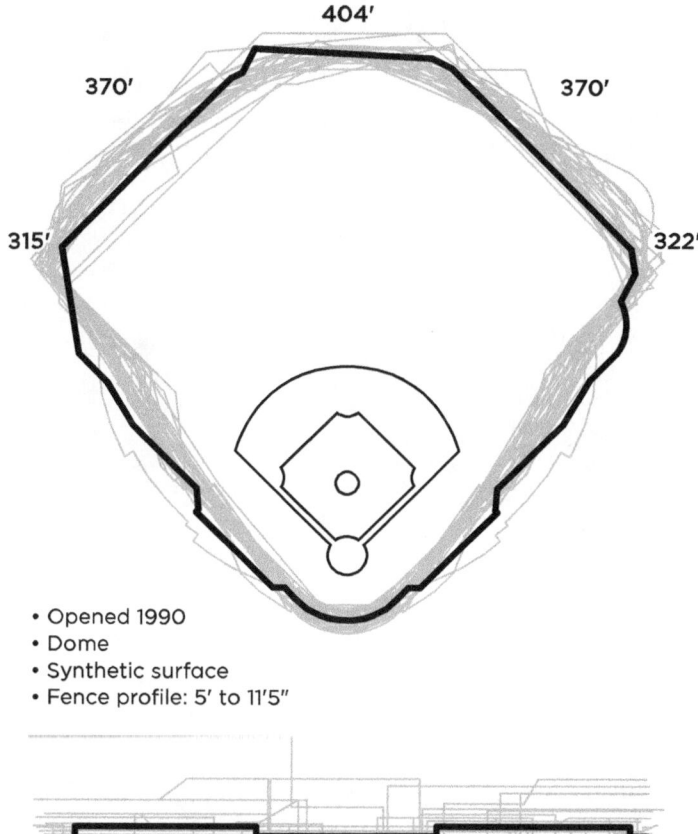

- Opened 1990
- Dome
- Synthetic surface
- Fence profile: 5' to 11'5"

Three-Year Park Factors

Runs	Runs/RH	Runs/LH	HR/RH	HR/LH
95	95	97	97	95

Rays Team Analysis

In 1921, a Swiss doctor named Hermann Rorschach published a book called *Psychodiagnostik*. In it, he explained how the images patients perceived in inkblots could offer insight into their personalities. The inkblot test became one of the primary projective personality tests—so-called because test-takers project their feelings onto these images—used by psychologists. When you look at this image do you see a butterfly or a wolf? Your response provides insight into your thought processes and, indeed, your worldview. Sports, and particularly fandom, tend to produce the same effect. The Tampa Bay Rays are baseball's Rorschach test. What you see when you look at them—their small payroll; their shifted fielders; their mix-and-match lineups—tells us something about you and your baseball *Weltanschauung*.

Maybe you see an easy-to-love scrappy melding of young talent, overlooked veterans and lottery-ticket minor-league signees rehabbing from their third Tommy John surgery. Despite the lack of pedigree, these guys somehow manage to be competitive. Over the past 13 seasons, the team has fallen below .500 just four times, two of those just barely under.

Maybe you see an innovative front office. The Rays were early adopters of an analytically driven approach to baseball. They shifted their infield before everyone was doing it—they'll throw a fourth outfielder out there, too, if the data suggest that's where the ball is going. Thanks to the Rays we have a whole new set of pitching roles. The opener. The bulk guy. The as of yet unlabeled lights-out reliever who is not the closer because you use him at the game's highest-leverage point and not exclusively in the ninth inning. They were the first (and perhaps still the only) team to put an analyst in uniform so he could be part of the coaching staff, ensuring that manager Kevin Cash is never more than two steps away from the best research possible.

Do you see a fox head or a jack-o-lantern in this inkblot? Maybe you see a team that is making baseball unwatchable. Their decisions are always data-driven. They aren't going to pay someone to be a good clubhouse guy. They don't care that you like watching name-brand workhorse starters grit their way through nine innings if data suggest that a no-name reliever provides the better eighth-inning matchup. The Rays have been accused of removing the "human element" (as though that no-name reliever is not also human!) or of playing an "aesthetically displeasing" brand of baseball.

Perhaps you see stingy owners who lead the perennial push to gain advantage over players who are one bad knee away from career's end. The Rays seldom compete aggressively for top free agents. They dump players as soon as they get the slightest bit expensive in arbitration. Solid major-leaguers like Corey Dickerson or Jake Odorizzi who provide value but not surplus value are disposed of for B-list minor leaguers. The very creativity that has marked the Rays' success also serves to undercut players' financial security. Pitchers, for example, get rewarded for metrics like games started and games saved; dispensing with starters and closers gives you an undifferentiated group of pitchers who will never have the leverage to demand higher salaries. And the Rays ability to succeed by taking advantage of hungry, low-salaried players creates a narrative further damaging to players' collective interests. Maybe you cringe when commentators note that some well-compensated but underperforming veteran "earns more than the entire Rays lineup!" the implication being that the underperforming veteran is the problem in this picture. Do you see a butterfly or a crab?

Or are you haunted by the monstrosity that appears if you try to see both? If those inkblots are ambiguous to disinterested observers, imagine how they look to emotionally invested Rays fans. Do they see a beloved home team giving some sense of belonging to a fragmented and footloose region? Or are the Rays just an asset from which out-of-town billionaires draw profit? This is a team that often plays great baseball, has provided Tampa Bay residents with elite performances and great sports moments. But thanks to the front office's approach to payroll, Rays fans will probably never get to see a star retire or a player go into the Hall of Fame with the "TB" on his cap. Rays fans do, indeed, root for laundry; it's almost a wonder they bother to stitch names on the back. And if the usual indignities of small-market fandom were not enough, the team's ownership announced last year that it intends to pursue a novel "sister city" concept in which the team will split its time between the not-very-good baseball market of Tampa Bay and the not-very-good baseball market of Montreal. Ownership has tried to sell this as a blessing, but fans recognize that it's just another quest for surplus value.

⚾ ⚾ ⚾

What is not up for interpretation is this: the 2020 Rays were a very good team. They won their division; their 40-20 record was second best in the majors. They won their Wild Card series with ease and triumphed in tense elimination games against the Yankees and Astros to reach the World Series. Yet they have no player under consideration for any end-of-season awards. Only manager Kevin Cash was recognized, handily winning the American League Manager of the Year Award.

The Rays' success should not have been a surprise. They finished 2019 with 96 wins. Pre-season, PECOTA projected them for 87 wins and the first AL wild card. They have a core of players who have proven their worth. Blake Snell was just a year off his Cy Young Award; Austin Meadows, Brandon Lowe and Charlie Morton had been 2019 All-Stars; Kevin Kiermaier has been a perennial Gold Glove center fielder whose spectacular catches and outfield assists are frequent highlight-reel features.

But the Rays won games with the help of many players who could not meet even the most generous definition of a "star." They did it, for the most part, with pretty good run prevention, giving up the fourth-fewest runs in the majors. And they did it with just enough hitting: 13th in team ops, 14th in home runs, 12th in runs scored.

As a team, they struck out a lot (highest rate in the majors), and walked a fair amount (fourth highest rate in the majors). Their 80 home runs were average for the league, but they outslugged the competition in the postseason with 34 home runs. Their offense was led by second baseman Brandon Lowe, who built on his strong 2019 rookie performance to show continued power that seems surprising given his slender build. He had a .285 ISO and wRC+ 150 through the regular season although he slumped badly in the postseason. His opposite was Yandy Díaz, known for arms that look like tree trunks, who, in an injury-shortened season, demonstrated a great eye but no power at all. His final offensive line included an impressive .428 OBP, alongside a head-scratching .079 ISO.

And in September they had Randy.

Randy Arozarena was acquired in a somewhat surprising offseason trade with the St. Louis Cardinals. The Rays are known for trading away established stars and getting cost-controlled prospects in return—Austin Meadows, Tyler Glasnow and Willy Adames are among the products of such transactions. But the trade with St. Louis involved Matthew Libertore, a hard-throwing 2018 first-round pick, a rare instance when the Rays traded a high-ceiling prospect for players able to help the team immediately. Arozarena, who had debuted late in 2019, joined the Rays at the end of August and started his assault on major-league pitching. He hit for average and power, and then chewed through pitchers named Cole, McCullers and Greinke to break several postseason records.

The Rays' success, however, was based on preventing runs more than scoring them. They fielded the ball well, although various defensive metrics are split on their team defense (SDI metrics used to assess Gold Glove awards loved their outfield but not the infield; as a team they were league best in UZR/150 but just fifth in DRS). They had some good starting pitching, but their starters did not shine in the regular season. No starting pitcher logged even 60 innings. Yonny Chirinos left for season-ending surgery; both Charlie Morton and Ryan Yarbrough lost weeks to injury. Tyler Glasnow's start was slowed by an early positive COVID-19 test. Blake Snell reported no health issues but seemed thrown off by the interrupted season and needed to be built up very slowly. Of their 60 regular season games, 11 (18 percent) were essentially bullpen days.

The success of the 2020 Rays largely rested on that bullpen, which posted a 3.37 ERA and 3.65 FIP. Their success is all the more impressive because some three-quarters of the projected Opening Day bullpen spent time on the Injured List, a good number of those (Chaz Roe, Colin Poche, Jalen Beeks and Andrew Kittridge) were deemed out for the season. Few of us had Ryan Sherriff, a 30-year-old journeyman who missed all of 2019, pitching meaningful innings in 2020. The bullpen wasn't, however, built entirely with spare parts. Nick Anderson had proven himself in 2019 and he had a strong if injury-shortened regular season with a 0.55 ERA, although his less effective postseason had many unfortunate repercussions. Other high-leverage arms included Diego Castillo, who struggled with control and got a bit lucky to end up with a 1.66 ERA, and Pete Fairbanks, whose 13.6 strikeouts-per-nine rate suggested he'd finally harnessed his swing-and-miss stuff. Despite the reliance on the pen, Cash was able to distribute the workload evenly and avoid overusing anyone; no pitcher was used three days in a row. Expanded rosters helped the Rays ensure that they always had a fresh arm on hand.

⚾   ⚾   ⚾

A team that is more than the sum of its parts needs a manager who melds those parts into an effective collective. As the unassuming manager of a small-market team Kevin Cash may (at least prior to his World Series appearances and Manager of the Year victory) not be known at all but if he's known for anything it's his willingness to pull his starter early. Cash has been the Rays manager for six seasons; in all that time Rays pitchers have pitched two complete games, both coming in the early years of his tenure. To be sure complete games are down across baseball (from 104 in 2015 to 45 in 2019), but Cash is at the cutting edge of this rotation management trend.

Cash has each game mapped out and knows more or less when he will turn it over to his bullpen. He believes strongly in the times through the order penalty, but he also looks at matchups as well as a starter's effectiveness. Game situation is always a factor. If his team is trailing a flailing starter may get more rope. If his team is winning he will maximize matchup advantage without regard to anyone's feelings. It's fair to guess that if we are to see another Rays complete game under Cash it will happen in a Rays loss.

He does not believe that "but he's dealing!" is a reason to change plans. In 2019, he pulled starter Ryan Yarborough one out short of a complete game 1-0 victory. As you might imagine, baseball observers had some feelings about that move, but Cash believed right-handed closer Emilio Pagán had a better shot at getting that last out against Seattle's right-handed hitting Domingo Santana. For a team in the wild card hunt, increasing the chances of winning was more important than the individual accomplishment of a complete game.

Those who have watched Cash, daily, escort grumbling starters from the mound in the fifth or sixth inning were therefore the least shocked by the postseason decisions that left the rest of the baseball world reaching for smelling salts. In must-win Game 7 of the ALDS, with Morton shutting down the Astros in the sixth inning, Cash went to his bullpen. The Rays went on to win that game (although it should be noted that Nick Anderson, who replaced Morton, did give up two runs). In a similar situation in must-win Game 6 of the World Series Cash infamously replaced an even more dominant Snell. This time, when Anderson faltered, it cost them the lead and eventually the game and the series. Cash has been criticized for that move; in an interview he said that even his young daughters are still angry at him. But the poor results in that moment don't discredit the process. When in the lead Cash always prefers to remove his starter before, and not after things start to fall apart. In that instance, one could argue, his mistake was not that he trusted the data that suggested removing Snell. It was that he ignored the data showing that Nick Anderson was not that Unlabeled Lights Out Guy at the moment, having been called on too many times. That game notwithstanding, results suggest his approach works more often than not. The 2020 Rays lost just once in the regular season when ahead after six innings.

⚾ ⚾ ⚾

Looking ahead to 2021, the Rays are well-positioned to contend. Pandemic-induced financial insecurity still hangs over baseball, and could be especially hard on teams with puny revenue streams, already operating on thinner margins. Conversely small-market teams could feel less impact on their bottom line since they earn less from the ticket sales and sponsorships affected by empty stadiums. This could level the financial playing field to where teams like the Rays can compete for free agents.

The Rays will have a core of young players returning in 2021 and may see the promotion of the next wave of budding stars, including top prospect Wander Franco. Their competitive window would seem to be wide open. But when the postseason ended, the Rays announced that they would not pick up the team options on catcher Mike Zunino and, most notably, Charlie Morton, who was scheduled to earn (and projected to deserve) $15 million. (Morton instead signed with the Braves, on a one-year deal worth that exact amount.) For two seasons Morton had been the highly respected and very effective elder statesman of the pitching staff, the man who won elimination games in both 2019 and 2020. A veteran with a World Series ring to his name, if anyone on the pitching staff had the standing to grumble about those Cash early hooks it was Morton, but he accepted Cash's choices with grace. Morton was even photographed sweeping up the clubhouse after his teammates' postseason clinching party left a mess. (Now there's a good clubhouse guy!) But remember, the Rays don't pay for clubhouse guys, or for veteran poise or even, apparently, for a still very good curveball.

Do you see dancing elephants or a tarantula? Charlie Morton, after all, is a 37- year- old who missed part of the shortened 2020 with a sore shoulder. Are the Rays the penny-pinching organization that let him walk, or the keen analysts who are already eyeing the unheralded non-roster invitee who will replace his production in 2021? ∎

—Elizabeth Strom is a writer and editor for DRaysBay.

Part 2: Player Analysis

PLAYER COMMENTS WITH GRAPHS

Willy Adames SS
Born: 09/02/95   Age: 25   Bats: R   Throws: R
Height: 6'0"   Weight: 210   Origin: International Free Agent, 2015

YEAR	TEAM	LVL	AGE	PA	R	2B	3B	HR	RBI	BB	K	SB	CS	AVG/OBP/SLG
2018	DUR	AAA	22	278	36	9	5	4	34	27	66	3	3	.286/.353/.412
2018	TB	MLB	22	323	43	7	0	10	34	31	95	6	5	.278/.348/.406
2019	TB	MLB	23	584	69	25	1	20	52	46	153	4	2	.254/.317/.418
2020	TB	MLB	24	205	29	15	1	8	23	20	74	2	1	.259/.332/.481
2021 FS	TB	MLB	25	600	72	23	2	21	73	61	198	3	2	.235/.318/.406
2021 DC	TB	MLB	25	551	66	21	2	19	67	56	182	3	2	.235/.318/.406

Comparables: Bobby Crosby, Jhonny Peralta, Addison Russell

The last hope for salvaging the David Price trade, Adames is holding up his end of the bargain by becoming a quality everyday shortstop. Always somewhat of a maverick in the field, he is a plus defender at the six who has cut down some of his riskier attempts. At the dish, Adames showed more power at the expense of his strikeout rate. We'll see if that's a legit trend or a byproduct of trying to make up for lost time. Yes, Wander Franco, Xavier Edwards and others are in the system, but don't overlook how good Adames has become.

YEAR	TEAM	LVL	AGE	PA	DRC+	BABIP	BRR	FRAA	WARP
2018	DUR	AAA	22	278	109	.367	1.5	SS(62): 2.4	1.5
2018	TB	MLB	22	323	100	.378	2.3	SS(75): -6.7, 2B(10): 1.7	1.2
2019	TB	MLB	23	584	93	.320	2.9	SS(152): 12.2	3.8
2020	TB	MLB	24	205	88	.388	1.2	SS(53): 2.5	0.5
2021 FS	TB	MLB	25	600	97	.334	-0.3	SS 2, 2B 0	1.7
2021 DC	TB	MLB	25	551	97	.334	-0.2	SS 2	1.6

Willy Adames, continued

Batted Ball Distribution

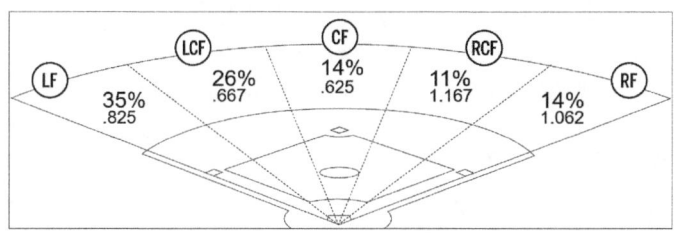

Strike Zone vs LHP   **Strike Zone vs RHP**

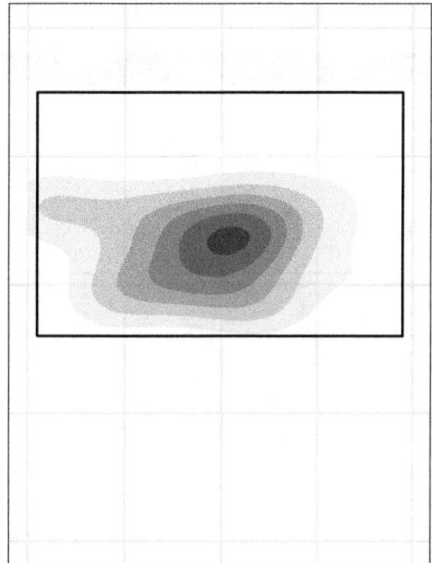

Tampa Bay Rays 2021

Randy Arozarena LF
Born: 02/28/95   Age: 26   Bats: R   Throws: R
Height: 5'11"   Weight: 185   Origin: International Free Agent, 2016

YEAR	TEAM	LVL	AGE	PA	R	2B	3B	HR	RBI	BB	K	SB	CS	AVG/OBP/SLG
2018	SPR	AA	23	102	22	5	0	7	21	6	25	9	3	.396/.455/.681
2018	MEM	AAA	23	311	42	16	0	5	28	28	59	17	5	.232/.328/.348
2019	SPR	AA	24	116	14	7	2	3	15	13	23	8	5	.309/.422/.515
2019	MEM	AAA	24	283	51	18	2	12	38	24	48	9	7	.358/.435/.593
2019	STL	MLB	24	23	4	1	0	1	2	2	4	2	1	.300/.391/.500
2020	TB	MLB	25	76	15	2	0	7	11	6	22	4	0	.281/.382/.641
2021 FS	TB	MLB	26	600	83	27	2	24	78	50	159	12	6	.249/.340/.451
2021 DC	TB	MLB	26	586	81	27	2	24	76	49	156	12	6	.249/.340/.451

Comparables: Brandon Jones, Dwight Smith, Chris Pettit

In the span of a few months, Arozarena emerged from relative obscurity to author one of the greatest postseasons in the history of the sport. He then followed up that run with something more serious and concerning: an arrest in Mexico after a domestic dispute with his ex-partner concerning their child. She later chose to not press charges.

YEAR	TEAM	LVL	AGE	PA	DRC+	BABIP	BRR	FRAA	WARP
2018	SPR	AA	23	102	193	.492	1.0	RF(12): 1.6, CF(6): -0.4, LF(5): 0.9	1.3
2018	MEM	AAA	23	311	81	.278	0.8	LF(49): -2.7, RF(18): 0.2, CF(10): -0.9	-0.5
2019	SPR	AA	24	116	160	.380	-0.5	CF(13): 0.9, LF(5): 0.0, RF(5): -0.7	0.9
2019	MEM	AAA	24	283	154	.404	-1.2	CF(25): -3.4, RF(20): 4.6, LF(14): 0.5	2.7
2019	STL	MLB	24	23	84	.333	-1.7	RF(6): -0.1, CF(5): 0.5, LF(1): -0.1	-0.1
2020	TB	MLB	25	76	115	.306	0.5	LF(14): -0.4, RF(3): -0.3, CF(2): 0.1	0.4
2021 FS	TB	MLB	26	600	117	.311	0.5	LF 0, CF 0	3.0
2021 DC	TB	MLB	26	586	117	.311	0.5	LF 0	2.8

Randy Arozarena, continued

Batted Ball Distribution

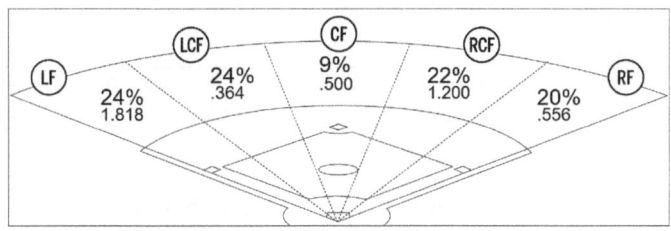

Strike Zone vs LHP   Strike Zone vs RHP

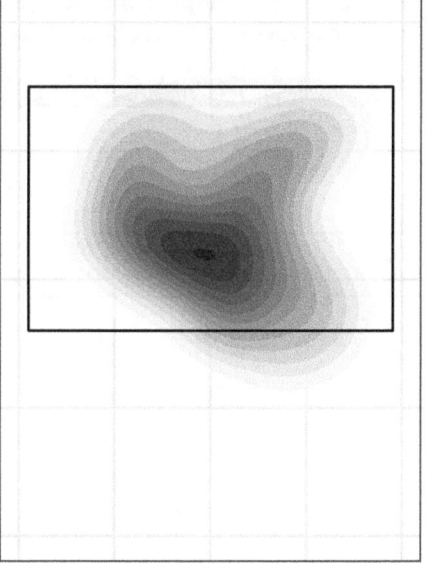

Mike Brosseau 3B

Born: 03/15/94 Age: 27 Bats: R Throws: R
Height: 5'10" Weight: 205 Origin: Undrafted Free Agent, 2016

YEAR	TEAM	LVL	AGE	PA	R	2B	3B	HR	RBI	BB	K	SB	CS	AVG/OBP/SLG
2018	MTG	AA	24	417	53	24	3	13	61	29	74	11	4	.262/.327/.449
2019	DUR	AAA	25	315	53	21	1	16	60	34	58	2	3	.304/.394/.567
2019	TB	MLB	25	142	17	7	0	6	16	7	39	1	0	.273/.319/.462
2020	TB	MLB	26	98	12	5	1	5	12	8	31	2	0	.302/.378/.558
2021 FS	TB	MLB	27	600	75	25	2	22	77	44	167	5	4	.240/.316/.420
2021 DC	TB	MLB	27	204	25	8	0	7	26	15	56	1	2	.240/.316/.420

Comparables: Andy Tracy, Luke Hughes, Danny Espinosa

In 2016, there were 1,216 players drafted. None of them were Brosseau. Proving that you can't keep a lion away from the hunt, he's turned himself into a solid little player with hard work and a little luck. He also provided one of the pivotal moments in the 2020 postseason when he delivered a series-clinching home run off Aroldis Chapman—the same Chapman who had directed a purpose pitch his way earlier in the way. Lions don't bring the cantaloupe, they go and get the antelope. For as long as Brosseau can pair his above-average stick with a versatile glove, he's going to have a spot on someone's roster.

YEAR	TEAM	LVL	AGE	PA	DRC+	BABIP	BRR	FRAA	WARP
2018	MTG	AA	24	417	114	.290	1.4	3B(64): 3.7, 2B(16): 0.0, 1B(10): -0.2	1.6
2019	DUR	AAA	25	315	134	.332	0.9	3B(32): -1.3, 1B(17): -1.1, 2B(7): -0.5	2.0
2019	TB	MLB	25	142	92	.345	1.0	2B(26): -0.5, 3B(18): -0.6, RF(6): -0.6	0.3
2020	TB	MLB	26	98	105	.412	-0.1	1B(12): 1.1, 3B(11): 2.0, 2B(9): -0.5	0.5
2021 FS	TB	MLB	27	600	100	.306	-0.2	2B 0, 3B 0	1.4
2021 DC	TB	MLB	27	204	100	.306	-0.1	2B 0, 3B 0	0.5

Mike Brosseau, continued

Batted Ball Distribution

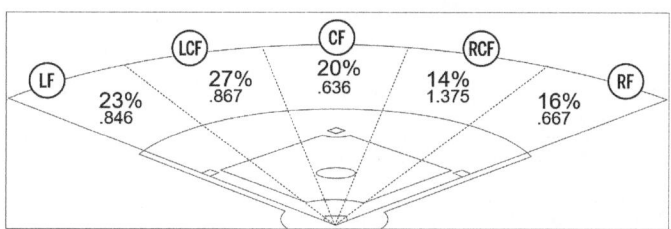

Strike Zone vs LHP   Strike Zone vs RHP

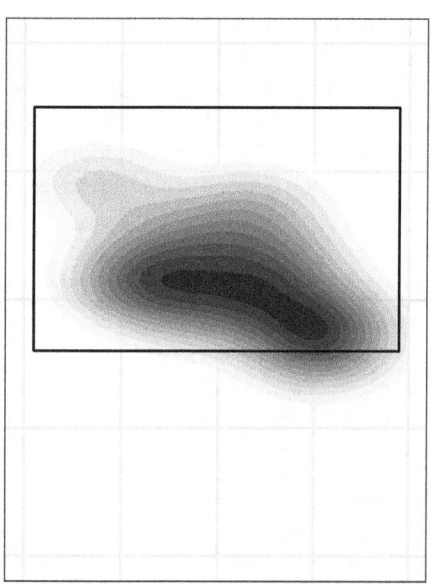

Type	Frequency	Velocity	H Movement	V Movement
● Fastball	75.0%	77.9 [53]	-4.8 [109]	-30.5 [57]
▲ Changeup	25.0%	63.5 [15]	-3.9 [142]	-53.4 [29]

Ji-Man Choi 1B

Born: 05/19/91 Age: 30 Bats: L Throws: R
Height: 6'1" Weight: 260 Origin: International Free Agent, 2009

YEAR	TEAM	LVL	AGE	PA	R	2B	3B	HR	RBI	BB	K	SB	CS	AVG/OBP/SLG
2018	RMV	AAA	27	163	17	9	0	5	23	32	31	1	0	.302/.436/.488
2018	DUR	AAA	27	86	9	4	0	2	14	11	18	0	0	.270/.360/.405
2018	MIL	MLB	27	32	4	2	0	2	5	2	14	0	0	.233/.281/.500
2018	TB	MLB	27	189	21	12	1	8	27	24	41	2	0	.269/.370/.506
2019	TB	MLB	28	487	54	20	2	19	63	64	108	2	3	.261/.363/.459
2020	TB	MLB	29	145	16	13	0	3	16	20	36	0	0	.230/.331/.410
2021 FS	TB	MLB	30	600	78	24	1	21	72	79	155	3	2	.230/.338/.411
2021 DC	TB	MLB	30	491	64	19	1	17	59	64	127	2	2	.230/.338/.411

Comparables: Derrek Lee, Tony Clark, Richie Sexson

The most interesting man in the Tampa Bay area (at least for several months of the year), Choi decided to hit right-handed in a big-league game in 2020 just to see what it was like. He went 3 for 11 during his experiment, including a memorable home run—that may not sound like much, but again, he did this on a whim. Choi later became the first Korean-born player to record a hit in the World Series. In between, he made a number of defensive highlight reels thanks to some, uh, aesthetically surprising flexibility that allows him to get into the split position for picks. You can understand, then, why Rays fans are smitten with Choi. The Rays Way often prioritizes efficiency above all else; we'll see if Choi's personality permits him to be the exception.

YEAR	TEAM	LVL	AGE	PA	DRC+	BABIP	BRR	FRAA	WARP
2018	RMV	AAA	27	163	143	.358	0.2	1B(38): -2.0, LF(1): 0.1	0.6
2018	DUR	AAA	27	86	119	.327	-0.9	1B(18): 0.2, LF(2): -0.0	0.1
2018	MIL	MLB	27	32	103	.357	0.3	1B(2): 0.0, LF(1): -0.0	0.1
2018	TB	MLB	27	189	110	.310	1.9	1B(1): -0.0	0.7
2019	TB	MLB	28	487	116	.303	-2.6	1B(103): -4.4	1.1
2020	TB	MLB	29	145	100	.291	-0.2	1B(38): -1.8	0.1
2021 FS	TB	MLB	30	600	106	.286	-0.5	1B -1, LF 0	1.1
2021 DC	TB	MLB	30	491	106	.286	-0.4	1B -1	0.9

Ji-Man Choi, continued

Batted Ball Distribution

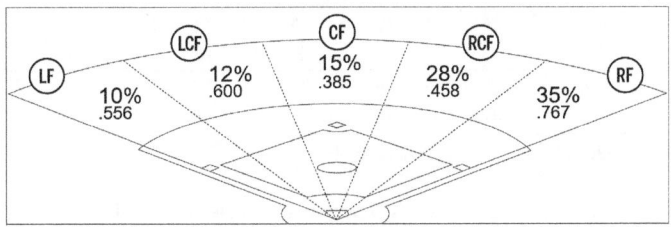

Strike Zone vs LHP   **Strike Zone vs RHP**

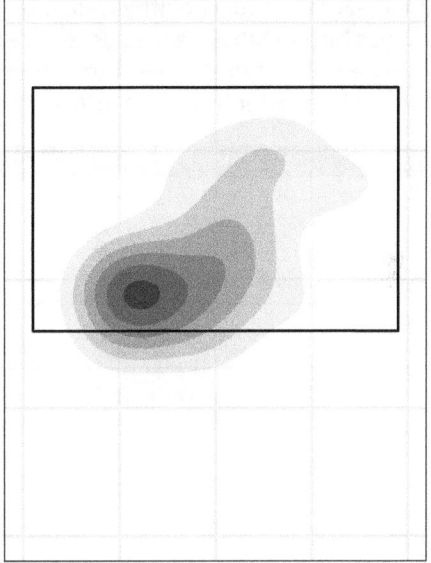

Yandy Díaz 3B

Born: 08/08/91 Age: 29 Bats: R Throws: R
Height: 6'2" Weight: 215 Origin: International Free Agent, 2013

YEAR	TEAM	LVL	AGE	PA	R	2B	3B	HR	RBI	BB	K	SB	CS	AVG/OBP/SLG
2018	COL	AAA	26	426	53	24	0	3	40	70	75	2	3	.293/.409/.388
2018	CLE	MLB	26	120	15	5	2	1	15	11	19	0	0	.312/.375/.422
2019	TB	MLB	27	347	53	20	1	14	38	35	61	2	2	.267/.340/.476
2020	TB	MLB	28	138	16	3	0	2	11	23	17	0	0	.307/.428/.386
2021 FS	TB	MLB	29	600	81	26	2	12	63	82	108	2	1	.271/.375/.401
2021 DC	TB	MLB	29	427	58	18	1	8	45	58	76	1	1	.271/.375/.401

Comparables: Brook Jacoby, Corey Koskie, Bill Sudakis

The Rays acquired Díaz before the 2019 season because of his penchant for hitting the ball hard. The idea was that if they could just get some lift in his swing, Diaz would greatly improve his slugging in part by smoking some pitches over the wall. It was a decent notion, and it worked somewhat in 2019. But in 2020? It did not work at all. Díaz put two-thirds of his batted balls on the ground, resulting in a negative launch angle. His offensive numbers were saved by a good average and a healthy walk rate, but it's a little hard to get juiced for a slow singles hitter without a true defensive home. Having big muscles makes for a cool aesthetic, but so does hitting home runs. The Rays would probably like more of the latter from Díaz in 2021.

YEAR	TEAM	LVL	AGE	PA	DRC+	BABIP	BRR	FRAA	WARP
2018	COL	AAA	26	426	144	.360	-2.6	3B(73): -9.6, 1B(12): 0.2	1.5
2018	CLE	MLB	26	120	102	.371	-2.0	1B(9): 0.2, 3B(9): 0.2	0.1
2019	TB	MLB	27	347	107	.288	-0.5	3B(50): -0.9, 1B(22): -0.1	1.2
2020	TB	MLB	28	138	106	.347	-0.4	3B(25): -1.0, 1B(2): -0.1	0.2
2021 FS	TB	MLB	29	600	118	.324	-0.7	3B -1, 1B 0	2.3
2021 DC	TB	MLB	29	427	118	.324	-0.5	3B -1, 1B 0	1.6

Yandy Díaz, continued

Batted Ball Distribution

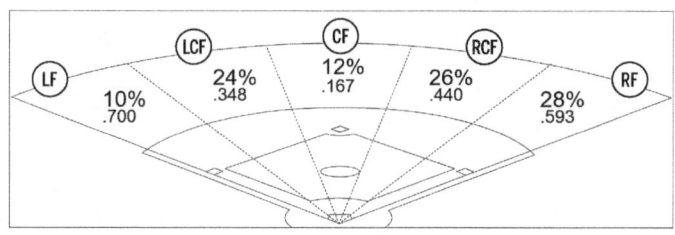

Strike Zone vs LHP　　　　　**Strike Zone vs RHP**

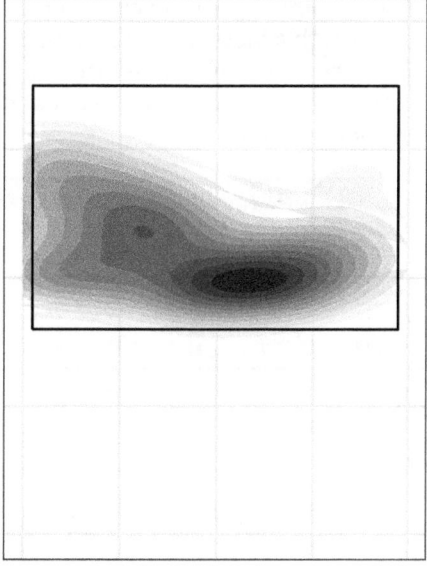

Rays Player Analysis - 25

Kevin Kiermaier CF

Born: 04/22/90 Age: 31 Bats: L Throws: R
Height: 6'1" Weight: 210 Origin: Round 31, 2010 Draft (#941 overall)

YEAR	TEAM	LVL	AGE	PA	R	2B	3B	HR	RBI	BB	K	SB	CS	AVG/OBP/SLG
2018	TB	MLB	28	367	44	12	9	7	29	25	91	10	5	.217/.282/.370
2019	TB	MLB	29	480	60	20	7	14	55	26	104	19	5	.228/.278/.398
2020	TB	MLB	30	159	16	5	3	3	22	20	42	8	1	.217/.321/.362
2021 FS	TB	MLB	31	600	65	22	6	16	66	50	151	20	9	.227/.301/.383
2021 DC	TB	MLB	31	415	45	15	4	11	46	34	105	14	6	.227/.301/.383

Comparables: Peter Bourjos, Austin Jackson, Cito Gaston

There's a case to be made that Kiermaier's 2020 was his best season in years. At minimum, he had his best offensive showing since 2017 thanks to a career-high walk rate. Kiermaier's approach was more disciplined than we're accustomed to seeing from him, and the gains in on-base percentage were enough to offset a similar uptick in strikeout rate. He also avoided the injured list for the first time since 2015. That's probably just a byproduct of the short season, as Kiermaier remains a walking—well, usually a diving or leaping—highlight reel in center field whose tendency to throw caution to the wind is both a blessing and a curse. His altered offensive philosophy suggests that he's capable of greater discernment on one end, though, so perhaps he's learning how to pace himself so that he does not erase himself from the lineup for weeks at a time.

YEAR	TEAM	LVL	AGE	PA	DRC+	BABIP	BRR	FRAA	WARP
2018	TB	MLB	28	367	76	.275	3.1	CF(88): 12.3	1.8
2019	TB	MLB	29	480	74	.267	1.9	CF(125): 6.0	1.0
2020	TB	MLB	30	159	77	.290	0.1	CF(46): -1.2	0.2
2021 FS	TB	MLB	31	600	85	.285	2.4	CF 7	1.7
2021 DC	TB	MLB	31	415	85	.285	1.7	CF 5	1.2

Kevin Kiermaier, continued

Batted Ball Distribution

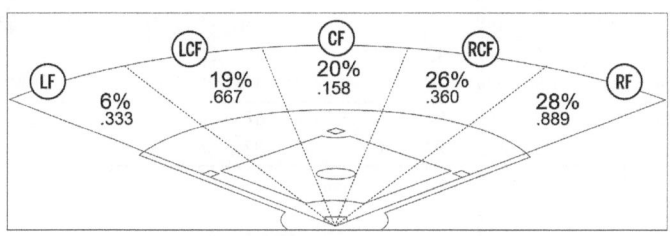

Strike Zone vs LHP   Strike Zone vs RHP

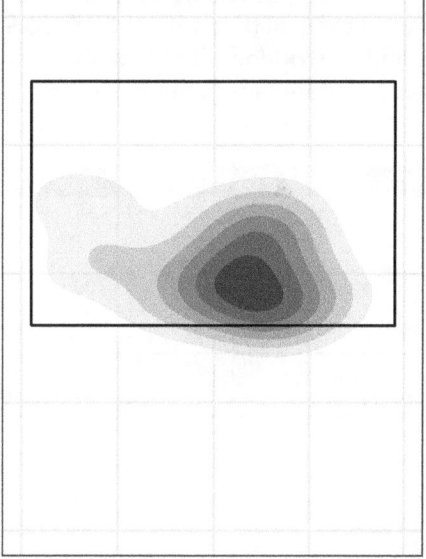

Brandon Lowe 2B

Born: 07/06/94 Age: 27 Bats: L Throws: R
Height: 5'10" Weight: 185 Origin: Round 3, 2015 Draft (#87 overall)

YEAR	TEAM	LVL	AGE	PA	R	2B	3B	HR	RBI	BB	K	SB	CS	AVG/OBP/SLG
2018	MTG	AA	23	240	37	17	1	8	41	35	55	8	2	.291/.400/.508
2018	DUR	AAA	23	205	36	14	0	14	35	22	47	0	1	.304/.380/.613
2018	TB	MLB	23	148	16	6	2	6	25	16	38	2	1	.233/.324/.450
2019	TB	MLB	24	327	42	17	2	17	51	25	113	5	0	.270/.336/.514
2020	TB	MLB	25	224	36	9	2	14	37	25	58	3	0	.269/.362/.554
2021 FS	*TB*	*MLB*	*26*	*600*	*84*	*26*	*3*	*30*	*87*	*57*	*169*	*2*	*2*	*.251/.332/.483*
2021 DC	*TB*	*MLB*	*26*	*568*	*79*	*24*	*3*	*28*	*82*	*54*	*160*	*2*	*1*	*.251/.332/.483*

Comparables: Yoán Moncada, Jason Bay, Pete Incaviglia

Lowe was an All-Star during the first half of 2019, and he played like one again during the half-but-actually-whole 2020 campaign. Postseason struggles aside, he was the Rays' best offensive player for most of the year. Indeed, over his last 551 plate appearances, Lowe has put together a line of .270/.347/.530 with 61 extra-base hits (31 of those being home runs)—not bad for someone with the ability to play at second base or in either corner outfield spot. He's locked into a multi-year deal that will pay him $20.5 million over the next four seasons, with a pair of club options after that. Because it's the Rays, there's a strong chance he's traded before those option decisions are due—just don't expect a deal to come anytime soon.

YEAR	TEAM	LVL	AGE	PA	DRC+	BABIP	BRR	FRAA	WARP
2018	MTG	AA	23	240	157	.360	2.1	LF(26): 1.8, 2B(24): -3.2	1.7
2018	DUR	AAA	23	205	171	.339	0.4	2B(31): 1.2, LF(13): 0.9	2.1
2018	TB	MLB	23	148	93	.279	0.8	2B(28): -0.6, LF(11): -0.3, RF(5): -0.1	0.3
2019	TB	MLB	24	327	107	.377	2.4	2B(69): 3.3, 1B(5): -0.8, RF(5): -0.5	1.7
2020	TB	MLB	25	224	127	.309	2.7	2B(44): -5.4, RF(7): 0.8, LF(5): -0.1	1.2
2021 FS	*TB*	*MLB*	*26*	*600*	*118*	*.310*	*-0.3*	*2B -1, RF 0*	*3.1*
2021 DC	*TB*	*MLB*	*26*	*568*	*118*	*.310*	*-0.3*	*2B -1, RF 0*	*2.9*

Brandon Lowe, *continued*

Batted Ball Distribution

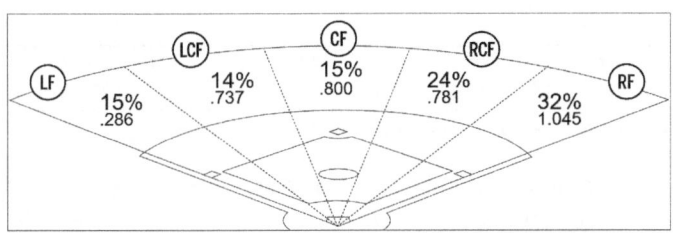

Strike Zone vs LHP   Strike Zone vs RHP

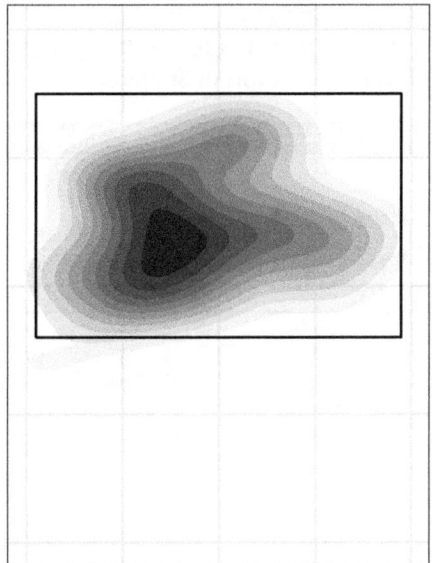

Manuel Margot CF

Born: 09/28/94   Age: 26   Bats: R   Throws: R
Height: 5'11"   Weight: 180   Origin: International Free Agent, 2011

YEAR	TEAM	LVL	AGE	PA	R	2B	3B	HR	RBI	BB	K	SB	CS	AVG/OBP/SLG
2018	SD	MLB	23	519	50	26	8	8	51	32	88	11	10	.245/.292/.384
2019	SD	MLB	24	441	59	19	3	12	37	38	88	20	4	.234/.304/.387
2020	TB	MLB	25	159	19	9	0	1	11	13	25	12	4	.269/.327/.352
2021 FS	TB	MLB	26	600	68	27	4	13	65	45	111	16	7	.250/.311/.394
2021 DC	TB	MLB	26	495	56	22	4	11	54	37	92	13	6	.250/.311/.394

Comparables: Ángel Pagán, Leonys Martin, Cory Sullivan

Margot once seemed destined to become a star in San Diego. He did just that last October—though, unfortunately for the Padres, he did it while playing neutral-site playoff games for the Rays. After homering once during the regular season, he jumped the fence five times in the playoffs, including three times during the AL Championship Series. Of course, the Rays weren't employing Margot because of his power; rather, they were employing him because of his speed and his defense. He delivered in both regards, stealing 12 bases in 16 tries and playing some quality D across the outfield. The Rays always seem to have an excess of outfielders, but Margot fared well enough to earn a second year playing on the turf in St. Pete.

YEAR	TEAM	LVL	AGE	PA	DRC+	BABIP	BRR	FRAA	WARP
2018	SD	MLB	23	519	84	.281	0.9	CF(136): -4.9	0.4
2019	SD	MLB	24	441	79	.272	4.5	CF(135): -4.6	0.5
2020	TB	MLB	25	159	86	.317	-0.4	CF(21): 2.2, LF(18): 1.5, RF(15): 0.2	0.4
2021 FS	TB	MLB	26	600	93	.292	1.4	CF 0, RF 1	2.0
2021 DC	TB	MLB	26	495	93	.292	1.2	CF 0, RF 1	1.4

Manuel Margot, continued

Batted Ball Distribution

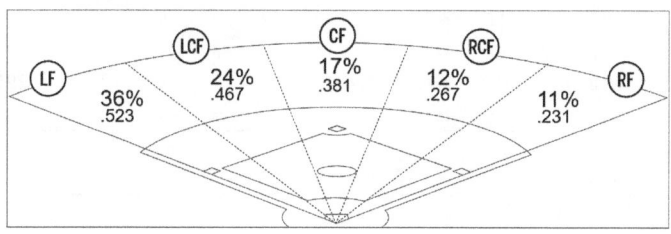

Strike Zone vs LHP Strike Zone vs RHP

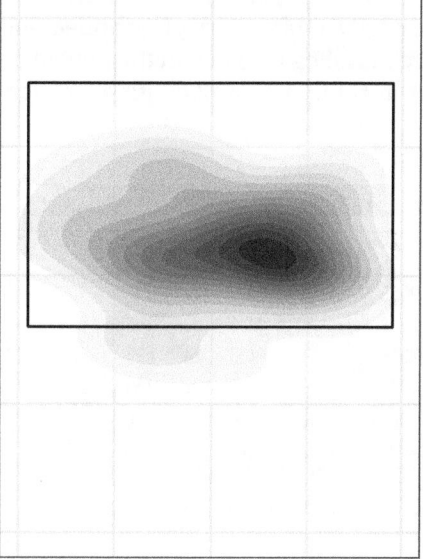

Austin Meadows RF

Born: 05/03/95 Age: 26 Bats: L Throws: L
Height: 6'3" Weight: 225 Origin: Round 1, 2013 Draft (#9 overall)

YEAR	TEAM	LVL	AGE	PA	R	2B	3B	HR	RBI	BB	K	SB	CS	AVG/OBP/SLG
2018	DUR	AAA	23	106	19	11	0	10	22	8	13	1	1	.344/.396/.771
2018	IND	AAA	23	179	27	13	0	2	21	9	24	11	1	.279/.318/.394
2018	TB	MLB	23	26	3	1	0	1	4	2	5	1	0	.250/.308/.417
2018	PIT	MLB	23	165	16	8	2	5	13	8	35	4	1	.292/.327/.468
2019	TB	MLB	24	591	83	29	7	33	89	54	131	12	7	.291/.364/.558
2020	TB	MLB	25	152	19	8	1	4	13	17	50	2	1	.205/.296/.371
2021 FS	TB	MLB	26	600	84	26	5	26	71	52	163	10	5	.239/.311/.453
2021 DC	TB	MLB	26	583	81	26	5	25	69	51	158	10	5	.239/.311/.453

Comparables: Yasiel Puig, Bobby Bonds, Danny Tartabull

Meadows tested positive for COVID-19 during the summer, sidelining him for the onset of the season. Perhaps he was still feeling the effects of the virus upon his return, or perhaps he had accumulated too much rust because of the odd circumstances. Whatever the case, he had a miserable season—a far cry from the 2019 performance that earned him MVP consideration. Meadows struck out in nearly a third of his plate appearances while losing nearly 100 points of ISO. We're willing to give him the benefit of the doubt, but another down season and he might find himself fighting for everyday at-bats on an ever-deep Rays roster.

YEAR	TEAM	LVL	AGE	PA	DRC+	BABIP	BRR	FRAA	WARP
2018	DUR	AAA	23	106	146	.311	-1.6	CF(17): -1.2, RF(4): -0.2, LF(2): -0.0	0.4
2018	IND	AAA	23	179	150	.314	2.4	CF(22): -1.5, LF(18): 0.1, RF(3): -0.4	1.3
2018	TB	MLB	23	26	95	.278	-0.1	RF(7): -1.4, LF(1): -0.0	-0.1
2018	PIT	MLB	23	165	95	.345	-1.1	CF(15): -0.7, RF(13): -1.1, LF(12): 0.0	0.1
2019	TB	MLB	24	591	134	.331	-3.5	RF(57): -3.5, LF(34): 4.6, CF(3): -0.0	3.7
2020	TB	MLB	25	152	87	.287	0.3	LF(23): -0.8, RF(4): 0.2	0.0
2021 FS	TB	MLB	26	600	104	.293	1.0	RF -2, LF 0	1.8
2021 DC	TB	MLB	26	583	104	.293	1.0	RF -2	1.4

Austin Meadows, continued

Batted Ball Distribution

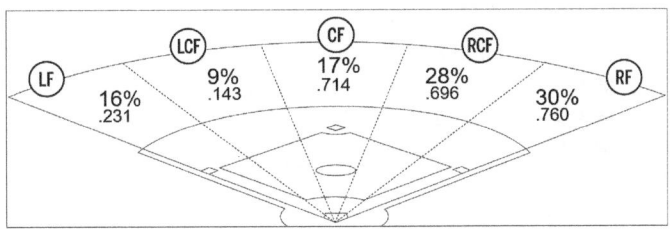

Strike Zone vs LHP

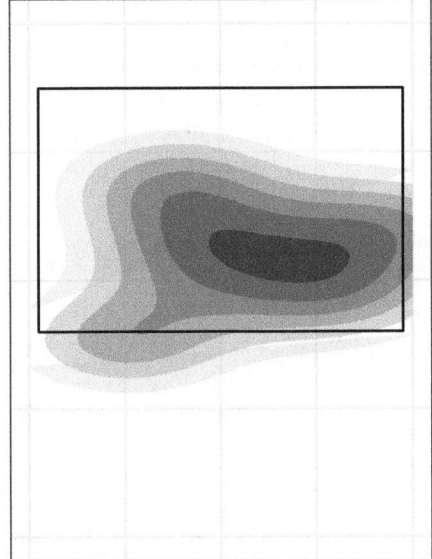

Strike Zone vs RHP

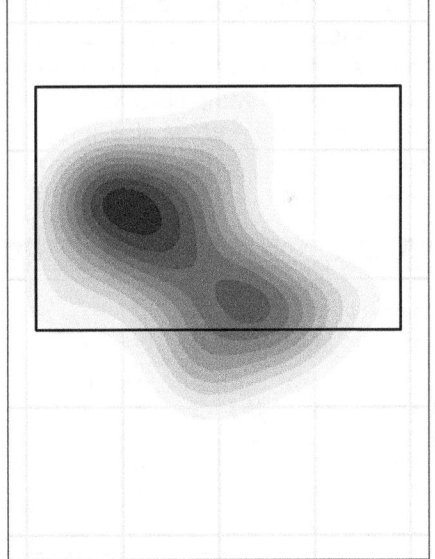

Brett Phillips RF

Born: 05/30/94   Age: 27   Bats: L   Throws: R
Height: 6'0"   Weight: 195   Origin: Round 6, 2012 Draft (#189 overall)

YEAR	TEAM	LVL	AGE	PA	R	2B	3B	HR	RBI	BB	K	SB	CS	AVG/OBP/SLG
2018	RMV	AAA	24	299	42	12	7	6	25	36	94	11	0	.240/.331/.411
2018	MIL	MLB	24	24	2	0	1	0	4	2	11	0	0	.182/.250/.273
2018	KC	MLB	24	123	13	4	2	2	7	9	50	1	1	.188/.252/.312
2019	OMA	AAA	25	414	75	8	13	18	54	72	118	22	1	.240/.378/.505
2019	KC	MLB	25	79	7	2	0	2	6	10	23	3	0	.138/.247/.262
2020	TB	MLB	26	25	2	0	1	1	3	5	7	3	0	.150/.320/.400
2020	KC	MLB	26	34	8	0	1	1	2	3	8	3	1	.226/.294/.387
2021 FS	TB	MLB	27	600	72	20	8	19	65	69	200	7	2	.219/.315/.400
2021 DC	TB	MLB	27	123	14	4	1	3	13	14	41	0	1	.219/.315/.400

Comparables: Gary Pettis, Kimera Bartee, Michael Bourn

Before Phillips became the unlikely hero of World Series Game 4, his most memorable moment with the Rays was when he defeated Randy Arozarena in a dance-off outside of Citi Field following Tampa Bay's division-clinching victory. Nearly a month later, the two combined for the Game 4 walk-off victory that left Rays fans doing the electric slide. The whole thing had to be extra special for Phillips, who went to high school just 14 miles away from Tropicana Field, and who had joined Tampa Bay at the deadline to serve as a pinch-runner and defensive sub. If nothing else, it reminded people why baseball is such a great game, even during otherwise trying times: from the unremarkable can come the incredibly fun.

YEAR	TEAM	LVL	AGE	PA	DRC+	BABIP	BRR	FRAA	WARP
2018	RMV	AAA	24	299	75	.346	1.1	RF(34): 2.9, CF(20): -1.8, LF(13): -0.2	-0.2
2018	MIL	MLB	24	24	42	.364	0.0	RF(7): -0.6, CF(5): 0.5, LF(2): -0.0	-0.1
2018	KC	MLB	24	123	45	.311	0.3	CF(23): 4.4, RF(9): 0.3, LF(1): -0.0	0.1
2019	OMA	AAA	25	414	108	.312	3.0	RF(63): 9.4, CF(32): -1.1, LF(3): 0.6	2.5
2019	KC	MLB	25	79	76	.167	1.2	CF(23): 1.0, LF(3): 0.5, RF(3): 2.0	0.5
2020	TB	MLB	26	25	92	.167	0.4	RF(9): -0.5, CF(4): 0.2, LF(3): 0.0	0.0
2020	KC	MLB	26	34	96	.273	-0.1	CF(11): 0.4, LF(4): 0.2, RF(4): -0.2	0.1
2021 FS	TB	MLB	27	600	95	.314	1.2	RF 3, CF 1	1.8
2021 DC	TB	MLB	27	123	95	.314	0.2	RF 1, CF 0	0.3

Brett Phillips, continued

Batted Ball Distribution

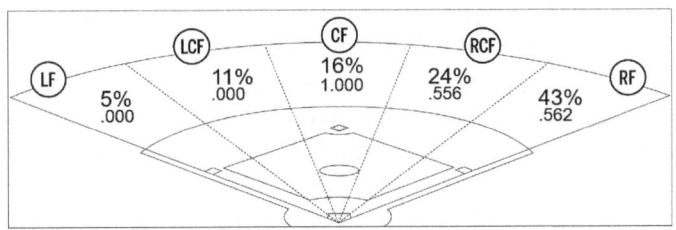

Strike Zone vs LHP   Strike Zone vs RHP

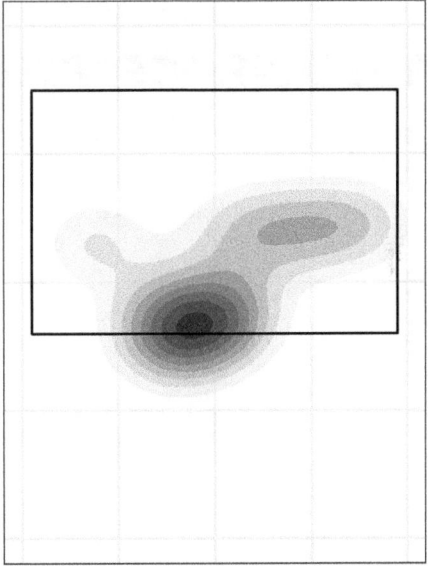

Yoshi Tsutsugo LF

Born: 11/26/91 Age: 29 Bats: L Throws: R
Height: 6'1" Weight: 225 Origin: International Free Agent, 2019

YEAR	TEAM	LVL	AGE	PA	R	2B	3B	HR	RBI	BB	K	SB	CS	AVG/OBP/SLG
2020	TB	MLB	28	185	27	5	1	8	24	26	50	0	0	.197/.314/.395
2021 FS	TB	MLB	29	600	74	22	1	17	71	69	165			.209/.307/.358
2021 DC	TB	MLB	29	408	50	15	1	11	48	47	112			.209/.307/.358

The Rays signed Tsutsugo to a two-year deal with the belief that his ample left-handed power would be great enough to warrant a spot in the lineup regardless of what position he played (and, to be certain, he isn't much of a fielder anywhere). The 29-year-old showed flashes of that plus pop and hit the ball hard with regularity, but it did not translate into enough actual production to cover his lack of defensive value. Additionally, his lack of speed limited the value of his 14 percent walk rate. By the playoffs he was relegated to mostly pinch-hitting duties and the occasional start at DH toward the bottom of the lineup. The Rays must be hoping the positive underlying metrics relative to hitting the ball hard will play out better over the course over a longer season in Tsutsugo's second year stateside.

YEAR	TEAM	LVL	AGE	PA	DRC+	BABIP	BRR	FRAA	WARP
2020	TB	MLB	28	185	101	.230	0.6	LF(16): -1.3, 3B(14): -1.5	0.1
2021 FS	TB	MLB	29	600	83	.269		3B -5, LF 0	-0.4
2021 DC	TB	MLB	29	408	83	.269		3B -3	-0.5

Yoshi Tsutsugo, continued

Batted Ball Distribution

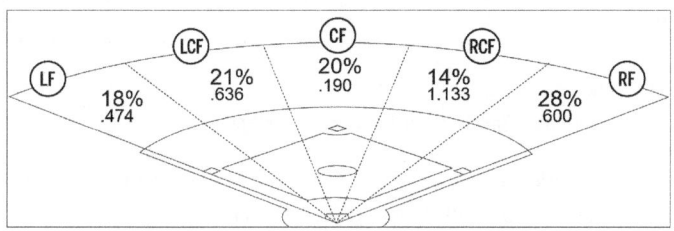

Strike Zone vs LHP   Strike Zone vs RHP

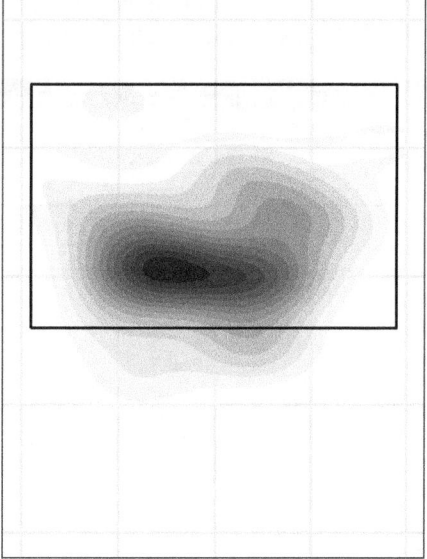

Joey Wendle 2B

Born: 04/26/90 Age: 31 Bats: L Throws: R
Height: 6'1" Weight: 195 Origin: Round 6, 2012 Draft (#203 overall)

YEAR	TEAM	LVL	AGE	PA	R	2B	3B	HR	RBI	BB	K	SB	CS	AVG/OBP/SLG
2018	TB	MLB	28	545	62	33	6	7	61	37	96	16	4	.300/.354/.435
2019	TB	MLB	29	263	32	13	2	3	19	14	47	8	3	.231/.293/.340
2020	TB	MLB	30	184	24	9	2	4	17	10	35	8	2	.286/.342/.435
2021 FS	TB	MLB	31	600	67	30	5	12	67	32	125	8	3	.256/.312/.400
2021 DC	TB	MLB	31	434	49	21	3	9	48	23	90	6	2	.256/.312/.400

Comparables: Robby Thompson, Tadahito Iguchi, Brandon Phillips

Wendle doesn't make much hard contact, but he makes a lot of contact in general and is a capable and versatile defender. His best role remains as a rover who can play three infield positions and some corner outfield while providing more bat-to-ball skills than most of his peers. Wendle is going to continue to draw the superlatives associated with generic-looking white players—gritty, scrappy and so on—yet that shouldn't detract from the value he's provided and should continue to provide to the Rays until they deem his cost to exceed his production. Given that he'll be heading for his second arbitration heading after the 2021 season, that could be, oh, any month now.

YEAR	TEAM	LVL	AGE	PA	DRC+	BABIP	BRR	FRAA	WARP
2018	TB	MLB	28	545	107	.353	3.7	2B(100): 5.8, 3B(20): 1.4, LF(16): -2.4	3.2
2019	TB	MLB	29	263	81	.272	-0.2	2B(48): 4.1, 3B(27): -1.1, SS(10): -0.0	0.6
2020	TB	MLB	30	184	91	.338	-0.6	3B(28): 2.3, 2B(20): 0.4, SS(10): 1.9	0.7
2021 FS	TB	MLB	31	600	92	.311	0.5	3B 1, 2B 1	1.4
2021 DC	TB	MLB	31	434	92	.311	0.4	3B 1, 2B 1	0.9

Joey Wendle, continued

Batted Ball Distribution

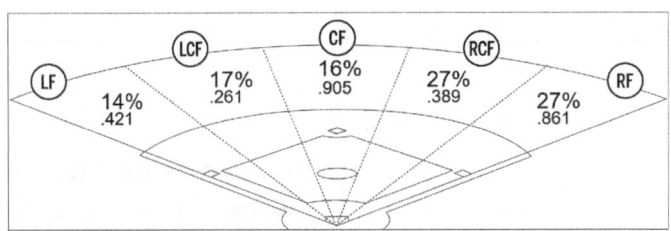

Strike Zone vs LHP   **Strike Zone vs RHP**

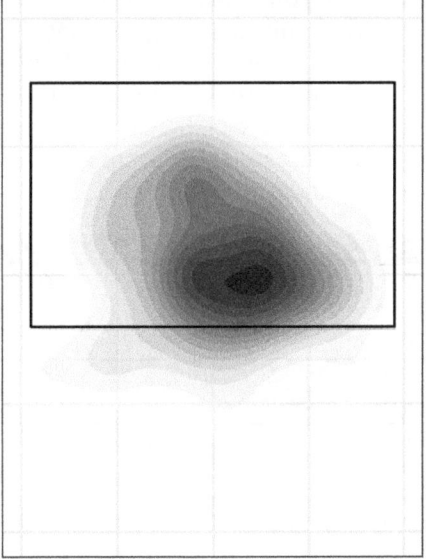

Mike Zunino C

Born: 03/25/91 Age: 30 Bats: R Throws: R
Height: 6'2" Weight: 235 Origin: Round 1, 2012 Draft (#3 overall)

YEAR	TEAM	LVL	AGE	PA	R	2B	3B	HR	RBI	BB	K	SB	CS	AVG/OBP/SLG
2018	SEA	MLB	27	405	37	18	0	20	44	24	150	0	0	.201/.259/.410
2019	TB	MLB	28	289	30	10	1	9	32	20	98	0	0	.165/.232/.312
2020	TB	MLB	29	84	8	4	0	4	10	6	37	0	0	.147/.238/.360
2021 FS	TB	MLB	30	600	74	24	1	26	74	49	234	0	1	.203/.286/.403
2021 DC	TB	MLB	30	275	34	11	0	12	34	22	107	0	0	.203/.286/.403

Comparables: Jarrod Saltalamacchia, Tyler Flowers, John Russell

YEAR	TEAM	P. COUNT	FRM RUNS	BLK RUNS	THRW RUNS	TOT RUNS
2018	SEA	14832	7.5	-1.1	0.4	6.8
2019	TB	11033	7.0	1.7	1.1	9.8
2020	TB	3613	-1.1	-0.6	0.1	-1.7
2021	TB	10822	4.6	0.3	-0.2	4.7
2021	TB	10822	4.6	-1.1	-0.2	3.2

Sometimes it doesn't pay to go home. The Rays had Zunino return to Florida for a second season with the hope that he would solve their seemingly never-ending quest for a legitimate starting backstop. In the end, they received two years of him hitting .161/.233/.323 with a strikeout rate nearing 40 percent. Despite a batting line that smelled like yesterday, Zunino was still able to make a cool $9 million. Though they declined his $4.5 million team option for 2021, the Rays brought him back into the fold for a less-cool $1.5 million less than that. The lesson here is to forget about having your kid learn to throw lefty; just toss them a catcher's mitt and a copy of Mike Fast's framing articles if you want to set them up for life.

YEAR	TEAM	LVL	AGE	PA	DRC+	BABIP	BRR	FRAA	WARP
2018	SEA	MLB	27	405	82	.268	-2.2	C(111): 6.4	1.6
2019	TB	MLB	28	289	56	.220	-1.5	C(89): 8.3	0.5
2020	TB	MLB	29	84	69	.206	-1.3	C(28): 0.8	-0.2
2021 FS	TB	MLB	30	600	86	.299	-0.9	C 7	2.1
2021 DC	TB	MLB	30	275	86	.299	-0.4	C 5	1.1

Mike Zunino, continued

Batted Ball Distribution

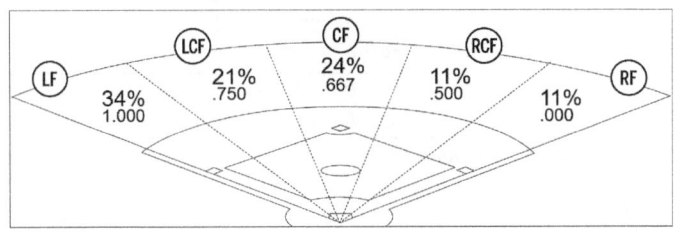

Strike Zone vs LHP   ### Strike Zone vs RHP

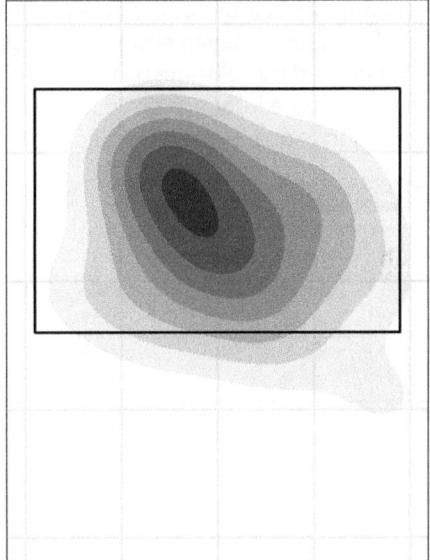

Nick Anderson RHP

Born: 07/05/90 Age: 31 Bats: R Throws: R
Height: 6'4" Weight: 205 Origin: Round 32, 2012 Draft (#995 overall)

YEAR	TEAM	LVL	AGE	W	L	SV	G	GS	IP	H	HR	BB/9	K/9	K	GB%	BABIP
2018	ROC	AAA	27	8	2	4	39	4	60	49	8	2.9	13.2	88	28.9%	.323
2019	MIA	MLB	28	2	4	1	45	0	43^2	40	5	3.3	14.2	69	28.0%	.368
2019	TB	MLB	28	3	0	0	23	0	21^1	12	3	0.8	17.3	41	32.4%	.290
2020	TB	MLB	29	2	1	6	19	0	16^1	5	1	1.7	14.3	26	20.7%	.143
2021 FS	TB	MLB	30	3	2	16	57	0	50	36	7	2.4	12.7	70	30.2%	.277
2021 DC	TB	MLB	30	3	2	16	62	0	66	47	9	2.4	12.7	92	30.2%	.277

Comparables: Ken Giles, Chad Green, Emilio Pagán

The Rays did not employ a traditional closer in 2020, but it was Anderson who was used most often in the highest-leverage situations. After striking out 42 percent of batters faced in 2019, he struck out a higher percentage last year with fewer walks and home runs allowed. The formula was simple: mix two-thirds fastballs with one-third curveballs and serve hot. That was regular-season Anderson, the one who also battled inflammation in his right arm. The other version, the October one, had a miserable playoff run, becoming the first pitcher to allow a run in seven straight appearances. He walked more batters and surrendered more home runs in the playoffs than he did during the regular season and he later admitted he was fatigued. Despite those circumstances, Anderson is one of the true relief aces in baseball when he's hearty and hale.

YEAR	TEAM	LVL	AGE	WHIP	ERA	DRA-	WARP	MPH	FB%	WHF	CSP
2018	ROC	AAA	27	1.13	3.30	55	1.7				
2019	MIA	MLB	28	1.28	3.92	70	0.9	97.3	55.9%	35.3%	
2019	TB	MLB	28	0.66	2.11	15	1.1	97.8	69.0%	43.1%	
2020	TB	MLB	29	0.49	0.55	81	0.3	96.4	65.0%	36.9%	
2021 FS	TB	MLB	30	0.99	2.47	61	1.3	97.2	61.1%	37.7%	48.4%
2021 DC	TB	MLB	30	0.99	2.47	61	1.8	97.2	61.1%	37.7%	48.4%

Nick Anderson, continued

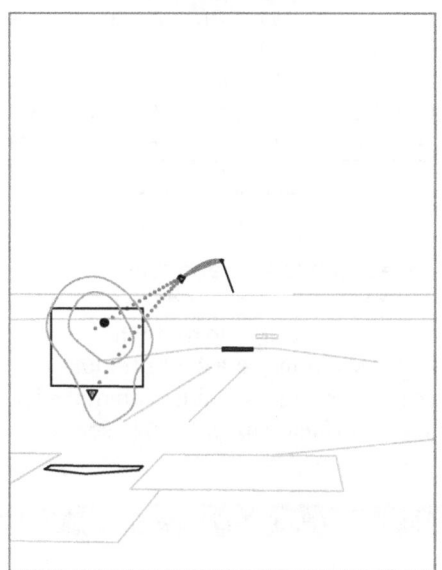
Pitch Shape vs LHH

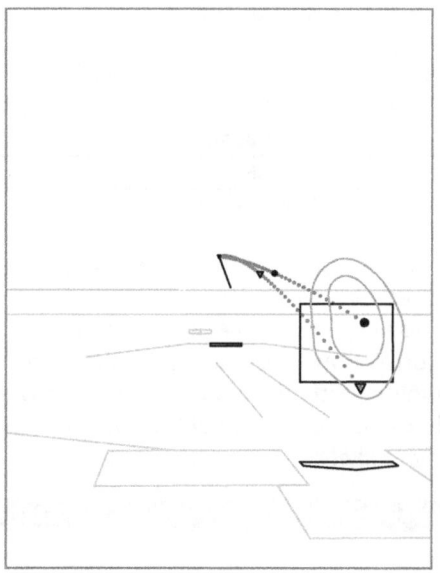
Pitch Shape vs RHH

Type	Frequency	Velocity	H Movement	V Movement
● Fastball	65.0%	95.4 [109]	-5.5 [106]	-10.4 [114]
▽ Slider	35.0%	84.6 [103]	1.9 [87]	-33.9 [100]

Jalen Beeks LHP

Born: 07/10/93   Age: 27   Bats: L   Throws: L
Height: 5'11"   Weight: 215   Origin: Round 12, 2014 Draft (#374 overall)

YEAR	TEAM	LVL	AGE	W	L	SV	G	GS	IP	H	HR	BB/9	K/9	K	GB%	BABIP
2018	WOR	AAA	24	5	5	0	16	16	87^1	70	10	2.6	12.1	117	39.8%	.300
2018	BOS	MLB	24	0	1	0	2	1	6^1	11	1	5.7	7.1	5	33.3%	.435
2018	TB	MLB	24	5	0	0	12	0	44^1	41	5	4.1	7.5	37	49.2%	.290
2019	DUR	AAA	25	0	1	0	3	3	10^2	8	2	3.4	8.4	10	39.3%	.231
2019	TB	MLB	25	6	3	1	33	3	104^1	115	12	3.5	7.7	89	46.0%	.329
2020	TB	MLB	26	1	1	1	12	0	19^1	21	1	1.9	12.1	26	41.2%	.408
2021 FS	TB	MLB	27	2	2	0	57	0	50	45	6	3.5	9.7	54	44.0%	.301

Comparables: Anthony Banda, Walker Lockett, Drew Anderson

Beeks looked different last season—and we aren't talking about his mustache. He scrapped his curveball in favor of more cutters and changeups, and he gained a tick on his fastball, allowing him to bump the mid-90s. Correlation does not imply causation, but Beeks' elbow gave way after just 19 innings with his new look. The Rays will cross their fingers that he can make it back before the end of the 2021 campaign. A resurfacing in early 2022 seems more likely.

YEAR	TEAM	LVL	AGE	WHIP	ERA	DRA-	WARP	MPH	FB%	WHF	CSP
2018	WOR	AAA	24	1.09	2.89	79	1.6				
2018	BOS	MLB	24	2.37	12.79	167	-0.2	93.6	47.4%	20.3%	
2018	TB	MLB	24	1.38	4.47	115	-0.1	93.6	42.5%	27.0%	
2019	DUR	AAA	25	1.12	4.22	81	0.3				
2019	TB	MLB	25	1.49	4.31	141	-1.7	94.2	43.6%	24.2%	
2020	TB	MLB	26	1.29	3.26	70	0.5	94.7	42.0%	32.9%	
2021 FS	TB	MLB	27	1.31	3.96	90	0.5	94.2	43.3%	26.0%	46.7%

Jalen Beeks, continued

Pitch Shape vs LHH

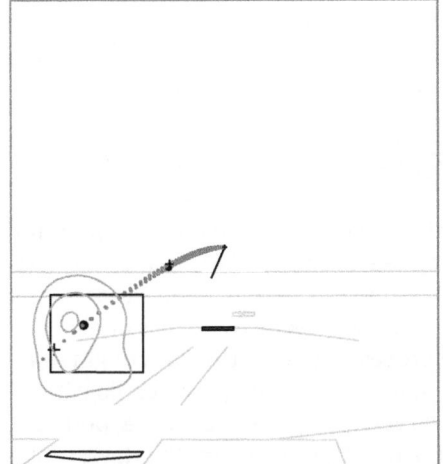

Pitch Shape vs RHH

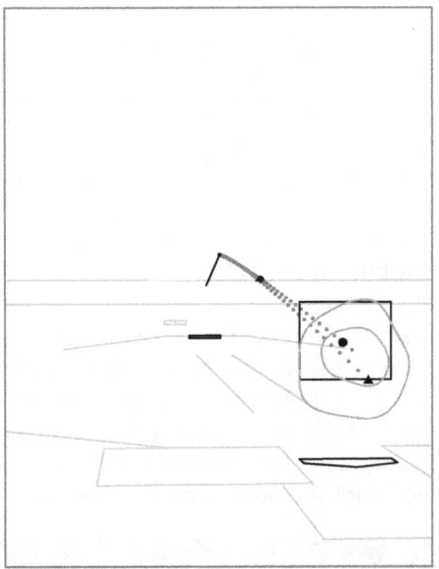

Type	Frequency	Velocity	H Movement	V Movement
● Fastball	42.0%	93.3 [102]	6.1 [103]	-12.6 [107]
+ Cutter	14.4%	86.8 [90]	-1.1 [95]	-26.2 [92]
▲ Changeup	43.6%	88.3 [112]	14 [88]	-24.1 [109]

Diego Castillo   RHP

Born: 01/18/94   Age: 27   Bats: R   Throws: R
Height: 6'3"   Weight: 250   Origin: International Free Agent, 2014

YEAR	TEAM	LVL	AGE	W	L	SV	G	GS	IP	H	HR	BB/9	K/9	K	GB%	BABIP
2018	DUR	AAA	24	0	1	4	19	0	26^1	15	1	2.4	10.9	32	58.6%	.246
2018	TB	MLB	24	4	2	0	43	11	56^2	36	6	2.9	10.3	65	46.0%	.229
2019	TB	MLB	25	5	8	8	65	6	68^2	59	8	3.4	10.6	81	55.1%	.302
2020	TB	MLB	26	3	0	4	22	0	21^2	12	3	4.6	9.6	23	59.3%	.176
2021 FS	TB	MLB	27	2	2	14	57	0	50	42	5	4.2	10.4	57	51.6%	.294
2021 DC	TB	MLB	27	3	3	14	62	0	66	55	6	4.2	10.4	76	51.6%	.294

Comparables: Keone Kela, Jordan Walden, Dominic Leone

    You can make the case that Castillo is the most underrated piece of the Tampa Bay pitching staff. He's now turned in three seasons of 141 ERA+ ball while pitching in high-leverage spots. Because Castillo has seldom been exposed to the ninth inning—he'll enter the year with just 12 career saves—he's unlikely to get expensive until late in the arbitration process. As such, the Rays might not feel the impulse to move him in the next year or two the way they could with some of the more famous members of their relief corps. In that sense, perhaps Castillo's position underneath the radar is a bit of a blessing for the Rays, though we doubt the burly fireballer feels that way himself.

YEAR	TEAM	LVL	AGE	WHIP	ERA	DRA-	WARP	MPH	FB%	WHF	CSP
2018	DUR	AAA	24	0.84	1.03	38	1.0				
2018	TB	MLB	24	0.95	3.18	82	0.9	100.4	54.1%	31.4%	
2019	TB	MLB	25	1.24	3.41	69	1.5	99.8	48.5%	32.7%	
2020	TB	MLB	26	1.06	1.66	83	0.4	98.3	35.3%	38.2%	
2021 FS	TB	MLB	27	1.31	3.66	85	0.7	99.6	46.6%	33.7%	47.5%
2021 DC	TB	MLB	27	1.31	3.66	85	0.9	99.6	46.6%	33.7%	47.5%

Diego Castillo, continued

Pitch Shape vs LHH

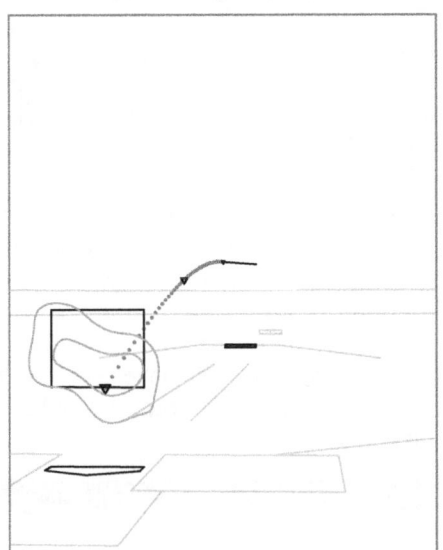

Pitch Shape vs RHH

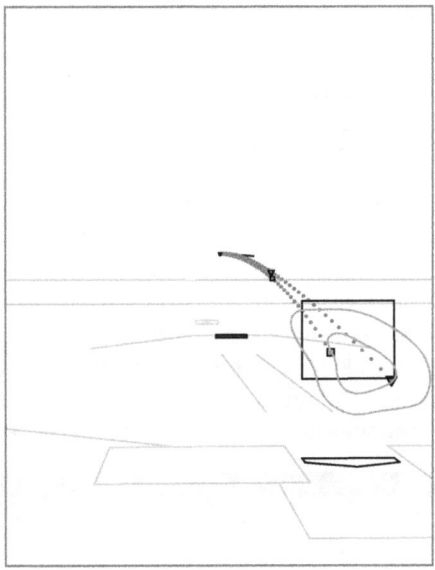

Type	Frequency	Velocity	H Movement	V Movement
☐ Sinker	33.8%	96.4 [120]	-15.4 [83]	-19.4 [104]
▽ Slider	64.7%	86.4 [111]	3.4 [93]	-31.6 [106]

Yonny Chirinos RHP

Born: 12/26/93 Age: 27 Bats: R Throws: R
Height: 6'2" Weight: 225 Origin: International Free Agent, 2012

YEAR	TEAM	LVL	AGE	W	L	SV	G	GS	IP	H	HR	BB/9	K/9	K	GB%	BABIP
2018	DUR	AAA	24	0	2	0	8	8	30²	35	7	2.1	9.1	31	49.5%	.326
2018	TB	MLB	24	5	5	0	18	7	89²	84	7	2.5	7.5	75	43.4%	.301
2019	TB	MLB	25	9	5	0	26	18	133¹	112	23	1.9	7.6	113	43.4%	.245
2020	TB	MLB	26	0	0	0	3	3	11¹	14	2	3.2	7.9	10	30.6%	.353
2021 FS	TB	MLB	27	2	2	0	57	0	50	48	7	2.4	8.2	45	41.8%	.288

Comparables: Joe Musgrove, Kevin Gausman, Trevor Williams

It looked like Chirinos was, at long last, going to be given a chance to perform as a traditional starter last season—an opportunity that he deserved, if you look at the stats. But Chirinos tried to succeed in the year 2020, so naturally, he landed on the injured list with a triceps issue after two turns through the rotation. He returned and made another start before a more serious ailment—a torn UCL—ended his 2020 and 2021 seasons in one swoop. He'll have celebrated two birthdays before making his next big-league pitch; we can only guess what he wishes for when he blows out those candles.

YEAR	TEAM	LVL	AGE	WHIP	ERA	DRA-	WARP	MPH	FB%	WHF	CSP
2018	DUR	AAA	24	1.37	5.28	97	0.3				
2018	TB	MLB	24	1.22	3.51	94	0.9	95.8	63.1%	24.1%	
2019	TB	MLB	25	1.05	3.85	87	2.0	96.2	56.8%	22.6%	
2020	TB	MLB	26	1.59	2.38	119	0.0	95.6	60.5%	30.1%	
2021 FS	TB	MLB	27	1.23	3.93	92	0.5	96.0	58.6%	23.7%	47.6%

Yonny Chirinos, continued

Pitch Shape vs LHH

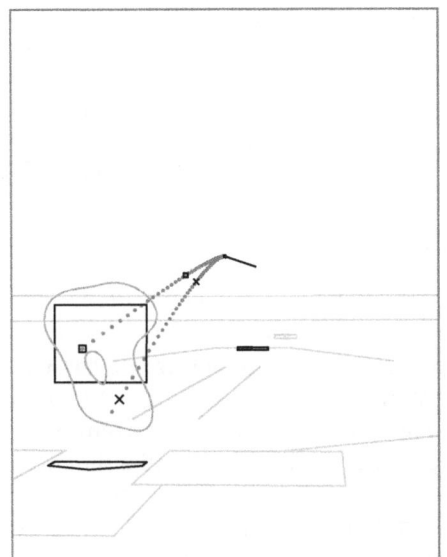

Pitch Shape vs RHH

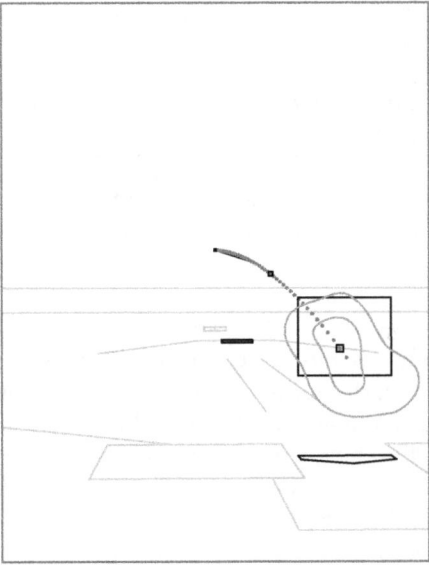

Type	Frequency	Velocity	H Movement	V Movement
● Fastball	13.2%	94.8 [107]	-9.8 [85]	-13.4 [105]
☐ Sinker	47.4%	93.1 [104]	-15.4 [83]	-19.3 [104]
✕ Splitter	23.7%	85.2 [100]	-7.9 [100]	-31 [95]
▽ Slider	15.8%	88.2 [119]	0.3 [81]	-25 [125]

John Curtiss RHP

Born: 04/05/93 Age: 28 Bats: R Throws: R
Height: 6'5" Weight: 220 Origin: Round 6, 2014 Draft (#170 overall)

YEAR	TEAM	LVL	AGE	W	L	SV	G	GS	IP	H	HR	BB/9	K/9	K	GB%	BABIP
2018	ROC	AAA	25	2	4	10	38	1	55¹	41	3	5.0	9.9	61	38.1%	.268
2018	MIN	MLB	25	0	1	0	8	0	6¹	8	0	5.7	9.9	7	10.5%	.421
2019	SL	AAA	26	2	0	1	13	0	21¹	20	4	5.5	12.2	29	41.5%	.327
2019	LHV	AAA	26	0	1	0	9	1	12¹	20	5	6.6	10.9	15	35.7%	.405
2019	LAA	MLB	26	0	0	0	1	0	2¹	2	0	11.6	3.9	1	50.0%	.250
2020	TB	MLB	27	3	0	2	17	3	25	21	3	1.1	9.0	25	42.0%	.273
2021 FS	*TB*	*MLB*	*28*	*2*	*2*	*1*	*57*	*0*	*50*	*44*	*7*	*3.7*	*9.8*	*54*	*38.5%*	*.285*
2021 DC	*TB*	*MLB*	*28*	*2*	*2*	*1*	*56*	*0*	*57.7*	*51*	*9*	*3.7*	*9.8*	*63*	*38.5%*	*.285*

Comparables: Phil Maton, Dan Altavilla, Jonathan Holder

Curtiss spent parts of the last three seasons in the majors with the Twins and Angels before fandangoing his way into the Rays depth chart in 2020. Due to myriad injuries to relievers, Curtiss was pressed into a regular role and served it well. He worked as both an opener and a standard reliever, striking out a batter per inning while keeping the bases relatively clean. Curtiss has a conventional approach, employing a fastball that creeps toward the mid-90s and a slider. Despite the lack of an offspeed item, he was actually more effective against lefties thanks to his control. To wit, Curtiss didn't walk any of the 40 left-handed batters he faced. Reverse splits without obvious explanations tend to be bugs more so than features. We'll see if Curtiss' is the exception.

YEAR	TEAM	LVL	AGE	WHIP	ERA	DRA-	WARP	MPH	FB%	WHF	CSP
2018	ROC	AAA	25	1.30	2.77	65	1.2				
2018	MIN	MLB	25	1.89	5.68	118	0.0	95.9	65.2%	26.0%	
2019	SL	AAA	26	1.55	5.91	80	0.5				
2019	LHV	AAA	26	2.35	10.95	190	-0.4				
2019	LAA	MLB	26	2.14	3.86	143	0.0	93.9	56.2%	26.3%	
2020	TB	MLB	27	0.96	1.80	84	0.4	95.9	56.5%	24.4%	
2021 FS	*TB*	*MLB*	*28*	*1.30*	*4.02*	*94*	*0.4*	*95.7*	*57.2%*	*24.7%*	*49.8%*
2021 DC	*TB*	*MLB*	*28*	*1.30*	*4.02*	*94*	*0.5*	*95.7*	*57.2%*	*24.7%*	*49.8%*

John Curtiss, continued

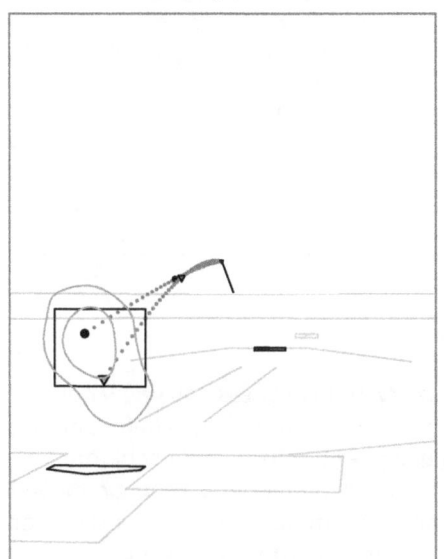
Pitch Shape vs LHH

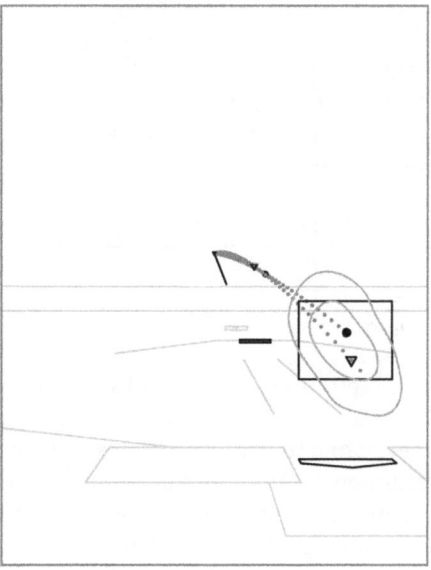
Pitch Shape vs RHH

Type	Frequency	Velocity	H Movement	V Movement
● Fastball	56.5%	94.2 [105]	-5.2 [107]	-12.7 [107]
▽ Slider	43.5%	85.4 [106]	4.7 [98]	-32.3 [104]

Oliver Drake RHP

Born: 01/13/87   Age: 34   Bats: R   Throws: R
Height: 6'4"   Weight: 220   Origin: Round 43, 2008 Draft (#1286 overall)

YEAR	TEAM	LVL	AGE	W	L	SV	G	GS	IP	H	HR	BB/9	K/9	K	GB%	BABIP
2018	SL	AAA	31	0	0	0	6	0	7^2	3	0	1.2	9.4	8	70.6%	.176
2018	CLE	MLB	31	0	0	0	4	0	4^1	7	0	2.1	8.3	4	31.2%	.438
2018	LAA	MLB	31	0	1	0	8	0	8^2	15	2	1.0	8.3	8	38.7%	.448
2018	MIL	MLB	31	1	0	0	11	0	12^2	14	0	5.7	10.7	15	54.3%	.412
2018	TOR	MLB	31	0	0	0	2	0	1^2	4	0	0.0	10.8	2	42.9%	.571
2018	MIN	MLB	31	0	0	0	19	0	20^1	12	2	3.1	9.7	22	49.0%	.204
2019	DUR	AAA	32	1	2	6	19	2	23^2	20	2	2.7	15.2	40	46.8%	.400
2019	TB	MLB	32	5	2	2	50	0	56	36	9	3.1	11.2	70	51.2%	.225
2020	TB	MLB	33	0	2	2	11	0	11	7	2	4.9	5.7	7	46.9%	.172
2021 FS	TB	MLB	34	2	2	0	57	0	50	42	5	3.8	10.2	56	47.9%	.289
2021 DC	TB	MLB	34	1	1	0	38	0	33	27	3	3.8	10.2	37	47.9%	.289

Comparables: James Hoyt, Fernando Salas, Brad Brach

Sometimes we laugh and sometimes we cry, but we guess you know now. Drake was poised to be one of the Rays' most important relievers before his arm knew when to say when. He experienced bicep tendonitis in August before returning in mid-September, then made the ALDS roster before being removed because of a right flexor strain. The Rays booted him from the roster altogether soon after, paving his path to free agency. At his best, Drake is a reverse-split right-hander that relies heavily on his splitter. If the elbow permits, he should be able to help out another club's bullpen. There is a chance, though, that it may be so far gone that we'll look back and say nothing was the same for Drake again.

YEAR	TEAM	LVL	AGE	WHIP	ERA	DRA-	WARP	MPH	FB%	WHF	CSP
2018	SL	AAA	31	0.52	1.17	74	0.1				
2018	CLE	MLB	31	1.85	12.46	57	0.1	93.8	48.1%	29.7%	
2018	LAA	MLB	31	1.85	5.19	69	0.2	94.2	47.1%	27.6%	
2018	MIL	MLB	31	1.74	6.39	56	0.4	93.8	49.0%	29.7%	
2018	TOR	MLB	31	2.40	16.20	43	0.1	93.6	58.3%	20.0%	
2018	MIN	MLB	31	0.93	2.21	75	0.4	93.7	41.0%	27.3%	
2019	DUR	AAA	32	1.14	4.94	50	0.9				
2019	TB	MLB	32	0.98	3.21	64	1.4	94.9	40.7%	36.1%	
2020	TB	MLB	33	1.18	5.73	106	0.1	92.7	48.0%	28.6%	
2021 FS	TB	MLB	34	1.26	3.47	81	0.8	94.3	43.1%	32.9%	48.5%
2021 DC	TB	MLB	34	1.26	3.47	81	0.5	94.3	43.1%	32.9%	48.5%

Oliver Drake, continued

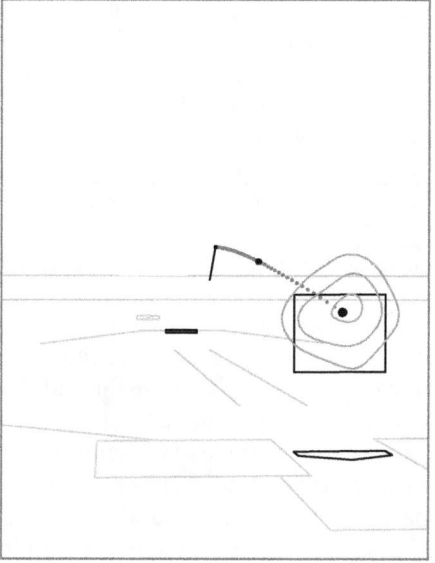

Pitch Shape vs LHH   **Pitch Shape vs RHH**

Type	Frequency	Velocity	H Movement	V Movement
● Fastball	46.9%	91.5 [97]	2.5 [144]	-13 [106]
✕ Splitter	49.7%	83.7 [93]	-1.9 [122]	-28.5 [103]

Pete Fairbanks RHP

Born: 12/16/93 Age: 27 Bats: R Throws: R
Height: 6'6" Weight: 225 Origin: Round 9, 2015 Draft (#258 overall)

YEAR	TEAM	LVL	AGE	W	L	SV	G	GS	IP	H	HR	BB/9	K/9	K	GB%	BABIP
2019	DE	HI-A	25	1	0	2	11	0	12^1	10	0	2.9	10.9	15	59.4%	.312
2019	FRI	AA	25	1	0	0	6	0	7^1	2	0	0.0	17.2	14	70.0%	.200
2019	NAS	AAA	25	0	0	0	7	0	6^1	10	1	2.8	15.6	11	27.8%	.562
2019	DUR	AAA	25	1	2	0	16	1	17^2	15	3	3.1	15.3	30	43.6%	.333
2019	TEX	MLB	25	0	2	0	8	0	8^2	8	4	7.3	15.6	15	42.1%	.267
2019	TB	MLB	25	2	1	2	13	0	12^1	17	1	2.2	9.5	13	42.9%	.390
2020	TB	MLB	26	6	3	0	27	2	26^2	23	2	4.7	13.2	39	48.4%	.350
2021 FS	TB	MLB	27	2	2	10	57	0	50	42	6	4.5	11.4	63	43.8%	.301
2021 DC	TB	MLB	27	3	3	10	62	0	66	56	8	4.5	11.4	83	43.8%	.301

Comparables: Michael Feliz, Phil Maton, Dovydas Neverauskas

Remember the scene in *Home Alone* when Macaulay Culkin puts the aftershave on his face? Remember his expression? That's the face Fairbanks makes anytime he's on the mound. Fairbanks throws really hard and is generally effective at getting outs, but his wide-eyed aesthetic is bound to inspire doubts from now until the day he hangs them up. The Rays probably won't mind too much so long as he keeps chucking his fastball in the upper-90s and breaking off nasty sliders. His command still isn't great and probably never will be, but he should continue to get looks in high-leverage situations—even if his eyes suggest he shouldn't.

YEAR	TEAM	LVL	AGE	WHIP	ERA	DRA-	WARP	MPH	FB%	WHF	CSP
2019	DE	HI-A	25	1.14	2.92	74	0.2				
2019	FRI	AA	25	0.27	0.00	35	0.3				
2019	NAS	AAA	25	1.89	11.37	75	0.2				
2019	DUR	AAA	25	1.19	5.09	51	0.6				
2019	TEX	MLB	25	1.73	9.35	77	0.1	99.2	51.5%	41.0%	
2019	TB	MLB	25	1.62	5.11	98	0.1	99.3	38.0%	29.1%	
2020	TB	MLB	26	1.39	2.70	66	0.7	99.1	57.6%	37.4%	
2021 FS	TB	MLB	27	1.34	4.02	90	0.5	99.1	52.9%	36.3%	44.0%
2021 DC	TB	MLB	27	1.34	4.02	90	0.7	99.1	52.9%	36.3%	44.0%

Pete Fairbanks, continued

Pitch Shape vs LHH	Pitch Shape vs RHH
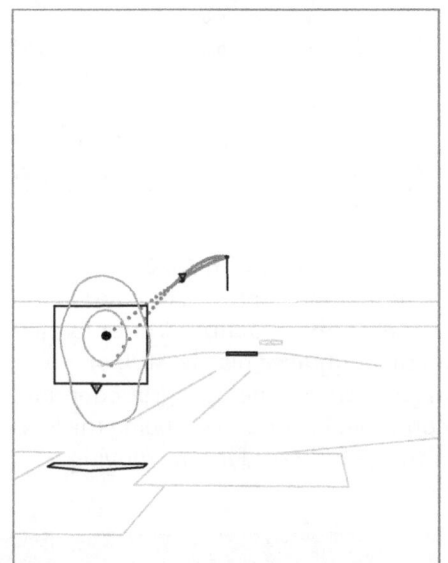	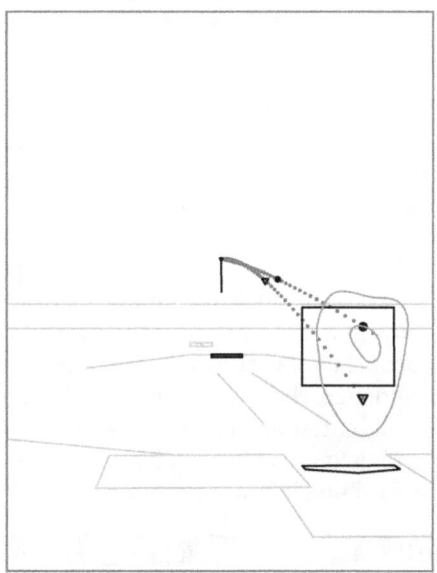

Type	Frequency	Velocity	H Movement	V Movement
● Fastball	57.2%	97.7 [116]	-0.2 [131]	-10.9 [112]
▽ Slider	40.7%	87.4 [116]	2.7 [90]	-36.2 [93]

Tampa Bay Rays 2021

Josh Fleming LHP

Born: 05/18/96 Age: 25 Bats: R Throws: L
Height: 6'2" Weight: 220 Origin: Round 5, 2017 Draft (#139 overall)

YEAR	TEAM	LVL	AGE	W	L	SV	G	GS	IP	H	HR	BB/9	K/9	K	GB%	BABIP
2018	BG	LO-A	22	6	1	0	10	10	60	41	1	1.5	6.3	42	56.1%	.234
2018	CHA	HI-A	22	3	3	0	9	7	50¹	51	4	1.6	6.8	38	44.7%	.301
2019	MTG	AA	23	11	4	0	21	17	127²	127	9	1.3	6.5	92	51.6%	.299
2019	DUR	AAA	23	1	3	0	4	3	21	24	6	3.4	6.9	16	65.2%	.286
2020	TB	MLB	24	5	0	0	7	5	32¹	28	5	1.9	7.0	25	63.9%	.250
2021 FS	TB	MLB	25	9	8	0	26	26	150	151	18	2.5	6.7	111	55.2%	.291
2021 DC	TB	MLB	25	5	4	0	19	11	78.3	79	9	2.5	6.7	58	55.2%	.291

Comparables: Nick Margevicius, David Peterson, Bernardo Flores Jr.

The cavalcade of injuries that disrupted the Rays rotation in 2020 unexpectedly pushed Fleming into big-league action. He proved that he was ready for it despite making just four appearances above Double-A prior to the season. Fleming showed poise and control that outpaced his raw stuff or experience. His low-90s sinker helped him generate a 64 percent grounder rate, and his cutter and changeup kept his platoon split in check. This being the Rays, Fleming figures to be used as a two-times-through-the-order-type moving forward—be it as a starter or as a "bulk guy."

YEAR	TEAM	LVL	AGE	WHIP	ERA	DRA-	WARP	MPH	FB%	WHF	CSP
2018	BG	LO-A	22	0.85	1.20	77	1.1				
2018	CHA	HI-A	22	1.19	4.11	70	1.1				
2019	MTG	AA	23	1.14	3.31	96	0.3				
2019	DUR	AAA	23	1.52	5.14	107	0.3				
2020	TB	MLB	24	1.08	2.78	86	0.5	92.2	83.6%	21.1%	
2021 FS	TB	MLB	25	1.28	3.87	91	2.2	92.2	83.6%	21.1%	45.7%
2021 DC	TB	MLB	25	1.28	3.87	91	1.1	92.2	83.6%	21.1%	45.7%

Josh Fleming, continued

Pitch Shape vs LHH

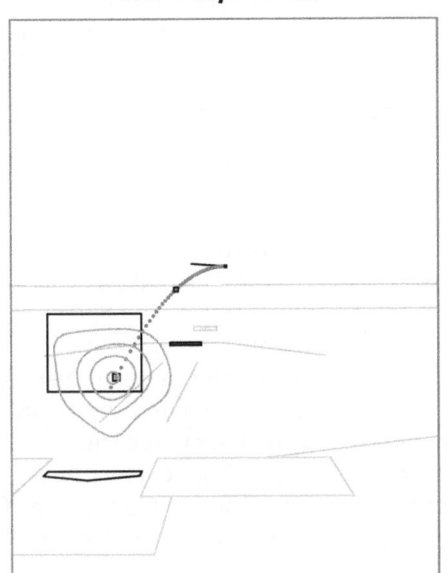

Pitch Shape vs RHH

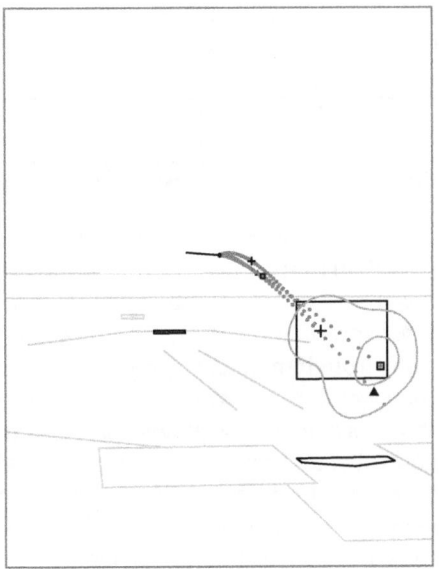

Type	Frequency	Velocity	H Movement	V Movement
☐ Sinker	53.2%	90.8 [92]	16.3 [76]	-24.6 [87]
+ Cutter	29.4%	85.7 [83]	-0.3 [90]	-28 [85]
▲ Changeup	15.5%	81.7 [87]	12.2 [98]	-35.7 [77]

Tyler Glasnow RHP

Born: 08/23/93   Age: 27   Bats: L   Throws: R
Height: 6'8"   Weight: 225   Origin: Round 5, 2011 Draft (#152 overall)

YEAR	TEAM	LVL	AGE	W	L	SV	G	GS	IP	H	HR	BB/9	K/9	K	GB%	BABIP
2018	TB	MLB	24	1	5	0	11	11	55^2	42	10	3.1	10.3	64	43.9%	.248
2018	PIT	MLB	24	1	2	0	34	0	56	47	5	5.5	11.6	72	55.9%	.321
2019	TB	MLB	25	6	1	0	12	12	60^2	40	4	2.1	11.3	76	50.0%	.265
2020	TB	MLB	26	5	1	0	11	11	57^1	43	11	3.5	14.3	91	40.0%	.281
2021 FS	TB	MLB	27	10	7	0	26	26	150	115	17	3.9	12.7	211	43.3%	.300
2021 DC	TB	MLB	27	9	6	0	25	25	132	101	15	3.9	12.7	186	43.3%	.300

Comparables: Lucas Sims, Robert Stephenson, Matt Wisler

There's a lot to like about Glasnow. He has an elite fastball and a Mjölnir curveball that allowed him to strike out nearly 40 percent of the batters he faced despite his predictability. And yet, so much still seems uncertain about his future production. When he's off with his stuff, even slightly, the plot can get away from him quickly. That's because Glasnow is reliant upon chases rather than well-located strikes. This approach works against most teams, but a team that has a few chess players can wait him out. It's easy to think that better control or an improved changeup is right around the bend, but he'll turn 28 before the next edition of this book comes out. As such, he seems more likely to keep up the Jekyll and Hyde thing than develop into the bonafide ace he looks to be when everything is clicking.

YEAR	TEAM	LVL	AGE	WHIP	ERA	DRA-	WARP	MPH	FB%	WHF	CSP
2018	TB	MLB	24	1.10	4.20	81	0.9	98.9	68.2%	28.1%	
2018	PIT	MLB	24	1.45	4.34	64	1.4	99.3	72.5%	29.7%	
2019	TB	MLB	25	0.89	1.78	56	2.0	99.3	67.3%	28.6%	
2020	TB	MLB	26	1.13	4.08	71	1.4	99.1	60.6%	32.8%	
2021 FS	TB	MLB	27	1.20	3.15	73	3.7	99.2	65.2%	30.5%	47.1%
2021 DC	TB	MLB	27	1.20	3.15	73	3.2	99.2	65.2%	30.5%	47.1%

Tyler Glasnow, continued

Pitch Shape vs LHH

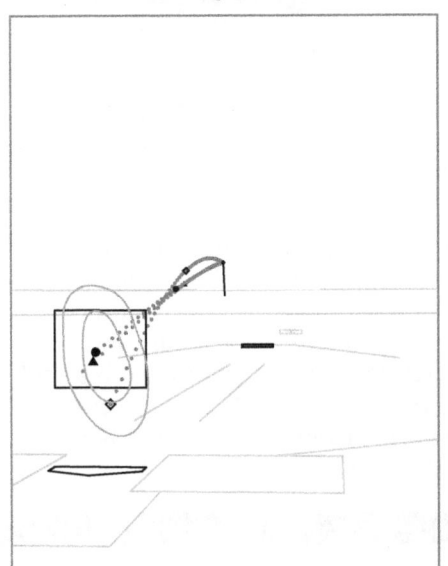

Pitch Shape vs RHH

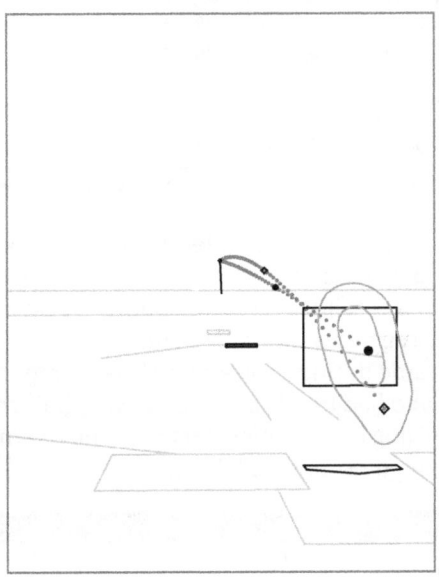

Type	Frequency	Velocity	H Movement	V Movement
● Fastball	60.6%	97.2 [115]	-0.5 [130]	-10.7 [113]
▲ Changeup	4.7%	91.3 [124]	-10.7 [106]	-20 [120]
◇ Curveball	34.8%	82.7 [116]	5.8 [93]	-52.7 [90]

Luis Patiño RHP

Born: 10/26/99 Age: 21 Bats: R Throws: R
Height: 6'1" Weight: 192 Origin: International Free Agent, 2016

YEAR	TEAM	LVL	AGE	W	L	SV	G	GS	IP	H	HR	BB/9	K/9	K	GB%	BABIP
2018	FW	LO-A	18	6	3	0	17	17	83^1	65	1	2.6	10.6	98	42.1%	.323
2019	LE	HI-A	19	6	8	0	18	17	87	61	4	3.5	11.7	113	40.2%	.278
2019	AMA	AA	19	0	0	0	2	2	7^2	8	0	4.7	11.7	10	19.0%	.381
2020	SD	MLB	20	1	0	0	11	1	17^1	18	3	7.3	10.9	21	34.7%	.326
2021 FS	TB	MLB	21	9	8	0	26	26	150	138	25	4.2	9.6	159	34.4%	.289
2021 DC	TB	MLB	21	5	4	0	40	6	63.3	58	10	4.2	9.6	67	34.4%	.289

Comparables: Jenrry Mejia, Taijuan Walker, Tyler Skaggs

Patiño had an underwhelming first go in the majors. He struggled with his control, seemingly validating the longstanding concerns evaluators had about his crossfire delivery resulting in command woes. In fairness to Patiño, his struggles were understandable (and often clustered, as eight of his 14 walks came during a miserable three-game stretch early on), as he was a 20-year-old who had barely pitched above A-ball entering the season. There's no sense giving up on youngsters this kind of arm talent or work ethic. He'll be back in due time, and he'll be good.

YEAR	TEAM	LVL	AGE	WHIP	ERA	DRA-	WARP	MPH	FB%	WHF	CSP
2018	FW	LO-A	18	1.07	2.16	75	1.7				
2019	LE	HI-A	19	1.09	2.69	55	2.4				
2019	AMA	AA	19	1.57	1.17	92	0.0				
2020	SD	MLB	20	1.85	5.19	110	0.1	98.6	64.8%	26.4%	
2021 FS	TB	MLB	21	1.40	4.65	102	1.2	98.6	64.8%	26.4%	46.6%
2021 DC	TB	MLB	21	1.40	4.65	102	0.3	98.6	64.8%	26.4%	46.6%

Luis Patiño, continued

Pitch Shape vs LHH

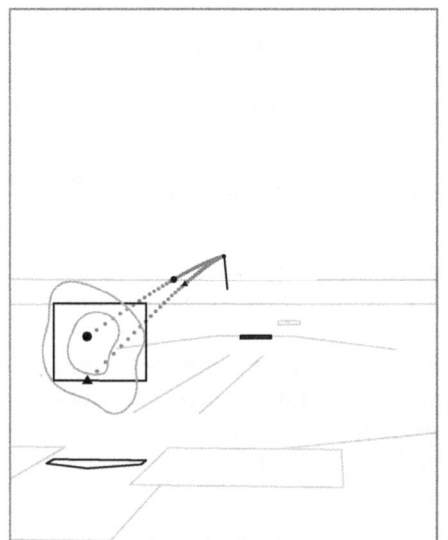

Pitch Shape vs RHH

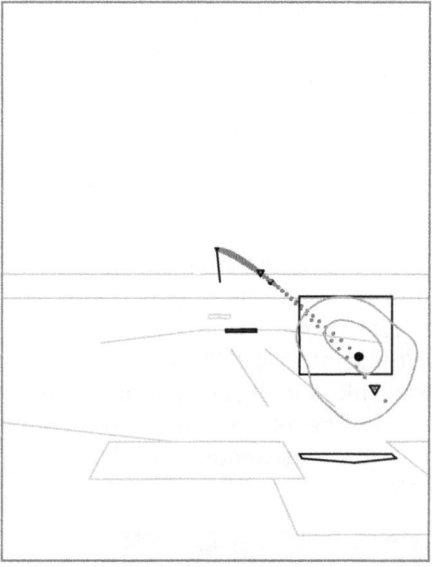

Type	Frequency	Velocity	H Movement	V Movement
● Fastball	64.8%	96.8 [113]	-1.3 [126]	-10.9 [112]
▲ Changeup	17.8%	89.1 [115]	-10.2 [108]	-21.3 [117]
▽ Slider	17.5%	84.6 [103]	10 [118]	-33.4 [101]

Cody Reed   LHP

Born: 04/15/93   Age: 28   Bats: L   Throws: L
Height: 6'5"   Weight: 230   Origin: Round 2, 2013 Draft (#46 overall)

YEAR	TEAM	LVL	AGE	W	L	SV	G	GS	IP	H	HR	BB/9	K/9	K	GB%	BABIP
2018	LOU	AAA	25	4	8	0	18	17	105²	109	13	2.6	8.9	105	45.1%	.329
2018	CIN	MLB	25	1	3	0	17	7	43	45	5	3.1	8.8	42	61.2%	.328
2019	LOU	AAA	26	1	2	0	18	0	20²	13	1	3.5	10.9	25	69.6%	.267
2019	CIN	MLB	26	0	0	0	3	0	6¹	6	0	1.4	9.9	7	76.5%	.353
2020	TB	MLB	27	0	1	0	11	0	12	11	2	6.0	9.0	12	44.1%	.281
2021 FS	TB	MLB	28	2	2	0	57	0	50	45	5	4.1	9.5	52	51.6%	.299
2021 DC	TB	MLB	28	2	2	0	56	0	52.7	48	5	4.1	9.5	55	51.6%	.299

Comparables: Robert Stephenson, Jeff Hoffman, Aaron Slegers

Reed, a large though rarely in-charge lefty, was one of Tampa Bay's big deadline acquisitions (yes, really). He made just two appearances with the Rays before a pinky injury ended his season and derailed any chance he had of turning into the 2020 version of Nick Anderson. Oh well. It's still easy to envision Reed blossoming into a more effective reliever than he's been thus far in his career. The main reason for that seemingly unearned optimism? A fierce slider that has consistently missed big-league bats, no matter the sample size or his role.

YEAR	TEAM	LVL	AGE	WHIP	ERA	DRA-	WARP	MPH	FB%	WHF	CSP
2018	LOU	AAA	25	1.32	3.92	79	1.9				
2018	CIN	MLB	25	1.40	3.98	97	0.4	94.9	50.2%	24.8%	
2019	LOU	AAA	26	1.02	2.61	57	0.7				
2019	CIN	MLB	26	1.11	1.42	65	0.2	96.2	55.2%	36.0%	
2020	TB	MLB	27	1.58	4.50	107	0.1	96.5	50.8%	29.4%	
2021 FS	TB	MLB	28	1.36	4.06	92	0.5	95.7	50.9%	27.8%	46.0%
2021 DC	TB	MLB	28	1.36	4.06	92	0.5	95.7	50.9%	27.8%	46.0%

Cody Reed, continued

Pitch Shape vs LHH

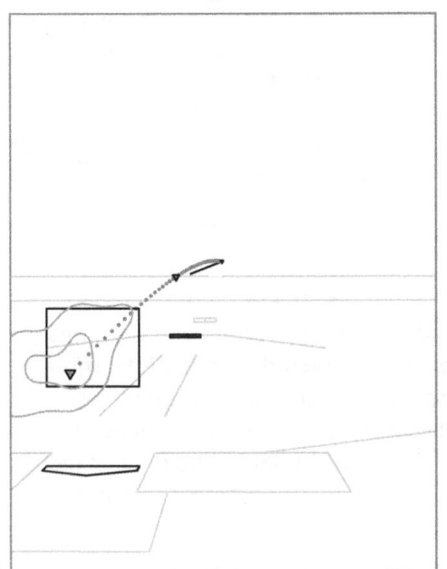

Pitch Shape vs RHH

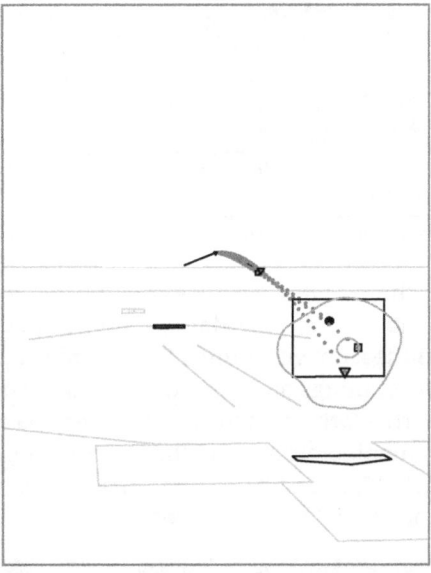

Type	Frequency	Velocity	H Movement	V Movement
● Fastball	28.0%	95.1 [108]	9.6 [86]	-17.2 [94]
☐ Sinker	20.3%	93.8 [107]	14.8 [88]	-22.9 [93]
▽ Slider	47.0%	87.3 [115]	-5.6 [101]	-32.2 [104]

Trevor Richards RHP

Born: 05/15/93   Age: 28   Bats: R   Throws: R
Height: 6'2"   Weight: 195   Origin: Undrafted Free Agent, 2016

YEAR	TEAM	LVL	AGE	W	L	SV	G	GS	IP	H	HR	BB/9	K/9	K	GB%	BABIP
2018	NO	AAA	25	3	2	0	6	6	39^1	31	4	0.9	8.5	37	47.2%	.262
2018	MIA	MLB	25	4	9	0	25	25	126^1	121	15	3.8	9.3	130	36.3%	.314
2019	DUR	AAA	26	0	0	0	3	3	5^1	4	0	6.8	13.5	8	33.3%	.333
2019	MIA	MLB	26	3	12	0	23	20	112	104	16	4.1	8.3	103	35.8%	.289
2019	TB	MLB	26	3	0	0	7	3	23^1	23	3	1.9	9.3	24	32.4%	.312
2020	TB	MLB	27	0	0	0	9	4	32	44	6	3.1	7.6	27	33.0%	.362
2021 FS	TB	MLB	28	9	8	0	26	26	150	144	26	3.5	8.7	144	37.2%	.289
2021 DC	TB	MLB	28	4	3	0	37	3	40	38	6	3.5	8.7	38	37.2%	.289

Comparables: Nick Pivetta, Kevin Gausman, Jon Gray

Richards, who will have to settle for being known as the *other* pitcher the Rays acquired from the Marlins at the 2019 deadline, filled a variety of roles in his first full season with Tampa Bay. His nine appearances included four starts, three bulk outings and a few old-fashioned mop-up assignments. He wasn't particularly great in any of those capacities, but he did start the clincher, which cemented his place in the team yearbook. Richards looks 47 and pitches like he's 37, but he'll be 27 until May—and employed as a utility arm until his changeup loses effectiveness.

YEAR	TEAM	LVL	AGE	WHIP	ERA	DRA-	WARP	MPH	FB%	WHF	CSP
2018	NO	AAA	25	0.89	2.06	56	1.3				
2018	MIA	MLB	25	1.39	4.42	79	2.5	92.2	54.8%	25.9%	
2019	DUR	AAA	26	1.50	1.69	83	0.1				
2019	MIA	MLB	26	1.38	4.50	116	0.1	92.4	42.3%	27.0%	
2019	TB	MLB	26	1.20	1.93	97	0.3	91.6	50.0%	24.2%	
2020	TB	MLB	27	1.72	5.91	125	-0.1	91.8	50.7%	25.7%	
2021 FS	TB	MLB	28	1.35	4.57	103	1.2	92.2	48.0%	26.2%	45.6%
2021 DC	TB	MLB	28	1.35	4.57	103	0.3	92.2	48.0%	26.2%	45.6%

Trevor Richards, continued

Pitch Shape vs LHH

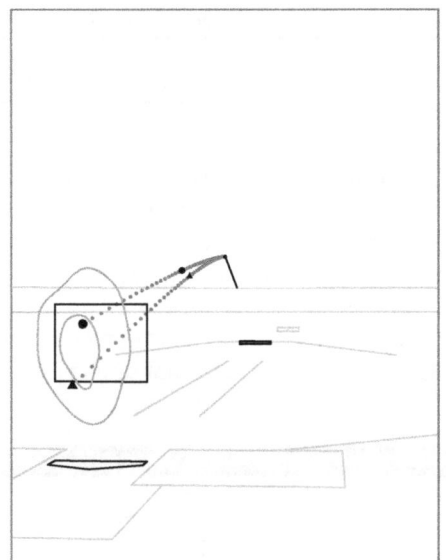

Pitch Shape vs RHH

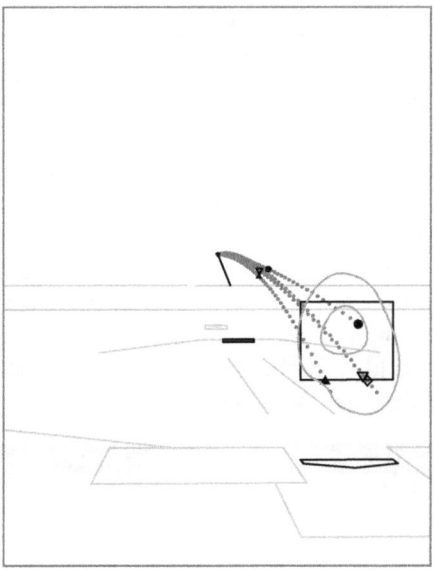

Type	Frequency	Velocity	H Movement	V Movement
● Fastball	50.7%	90.7 [94]	-6.1 [103]	-12.9 [107]
▲ Changeup	31.1%	82.7 [90]	-13.6 [90]	-27.6 [100]
▽ Slider	10.8%	83.4 [98]	3.8 [95]	-32.8 [103]
◇ Curveball	7.5%	81.8 [113]	2.6 [80]	-38.1 [123]

Tampa Bay Rays 2021

Will Sherriff LHP
Born: 02/02/02   Age: 19   Bats: L   Throws: L
Height: 6'0"   Weight: 170   Origin: Round 28, 2011 Draft (#860 overall)

YEAR	TEAM	LVL	AGE	W	L	SV	G	GS	IP	H	HR	BB/9	K/9	K	GB%	BABIP
2018	STL	MLB	28	0	0	0	5	0	5²	8	1	3.2	4.8	3	57.1%	.350
2020	TB	MLB	30	1	0	1	10	0	9²	6	0	1.9	1.9	2	56.7%	.200
2021 FS	TB	MLB	19	2	2	0	57	0	50	52	6	2.4	5.8	32	52.3%	.292
2021 DC	TB	MLB	19	2	2	0	56	0	39.3	41	4	2.4	5.8	25	52.3%	.292

Comparables: Buddy Baumann, Scott Alexander, Andrew Kittredge

Sherriff returned to the majors for the first time since undergoing elbow surgery. Partially because of the three-batter rule, he faced more righties than lefties but was effective all the same, using a fastball nearly 80 percent of the time. He backed up his modest heater with a low-80s slider and he even attempted to toss a changeup for the first time. Sherriff was not scored upon in 10 regular season appearances, and he added two more scoreless frames in the World Series as the capper to his encouraging year. If he keeps that up, he just might earn a badge.

YEAR	TEAM	LVL	AGE	WHIP	ERA	DRA-	WARP	MPH	FB%	WHF	CSP
2018	STL	MLB	28	1.76	6.35	138	-0.1	92.3	72.8%	15.0%	
2020	TB	MLB	30	0.83	0.00	105	0.1	92.7	80.2%	10.0%	
2021 FS	TB	MLB	19	1.31	4.15	96	0.4	92.6	78.6%	11.1%	50.5%
2021 DC	TB	MLB	19	1.31	4.15	96	0.3	92.6	78.6%	11.1%	50.5%

Will Sherriff, continued

Pitch Shape vs LHH

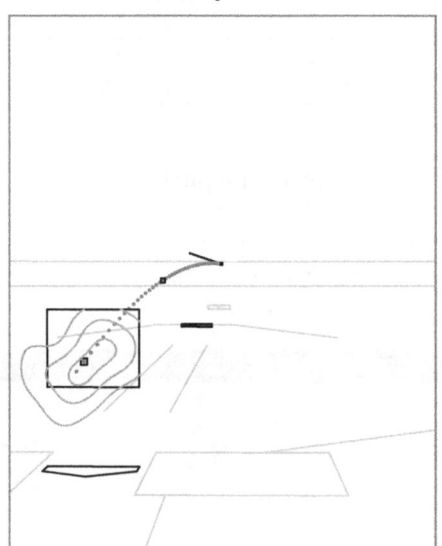

Pitch Shape vs RHH

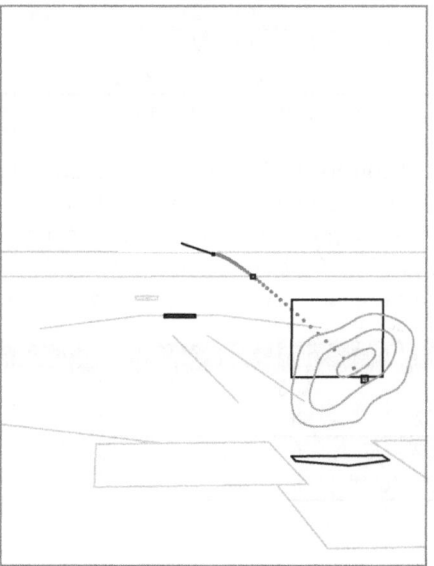

Type	Frequency	Velocity	H Movement	V Movement
☐ Sinker	80.2%	91.1 [93]	15.5 [82]	-28.3 [75]
▽ Slider	17.5%	80.8 [86]	-8.8 [114]	-36.7 [92]

Tampa Bay Rays 2021

Ryan Thompson   RHP
Born: 06/26/92   Age: 29   Bats: R   Throws: R
Height: 6'5"   Weight: 210   Origin: Round 23, 2014 Draft (#676 overall)

YEAR	TEAM	LVL	AGE	W	L	SV	G	GS	IP	H	HR	BB/9	K/9	K	GB%	BABIP
2019	MTG	AA	27	1	1	0	14	5	20¹	24	1	2.7	8.9	20	44.4%	.371
2020	TB	MLB	28	1	2	1	25	1	26¹	29	4	2.7	7.9	23	59.0%	.316
2021 FS	TB	MLB	29	2	2	0	57	0	50	48	6	3.1	8.1	44	51.2%	.295
2021 DC	TB	MLB	29	3	3	0	62	0	52.7	51	6	3.1	8.1	47	51.2%	.295

Comparables: Chris Leroux, Josh Lueke, Eric Yardley

Thompson checks all the buzzword boxes associated with pitching. At 6-foot-5, 200 pounds, he's both "long" and "lanky." His delivery, a violent sidearm motion, makes him "deceptive." And, he's a classic "sinker-slider" right-hander to boot. In the older days, he'd probably be called a "specialist." In this era, he might end up being referred to as an "up-and-down" arm instead.

YEAR	TEAM	LVL	AGE	WHIP	ERA	DRA-	WARP	MPH	FB%	WHF	CSP
2019	MTG	AA	27	1.48	3.10	120	-0.3				
2020	TB	MLB	28	1.41	4.44	81	0.5	93.6	60.9%	22.2%	
2021 FS	TB	MLB	29	1.32	4.12	94	0.4	93.6	60.9%	22.2%	52.8%
2021 DC	TB	MLB	29	1.32	4.12	94	0.4	93.6	60.9%	22.2%	52.8%

Ryan Thompson, continued

Pitch Shape vs LHH

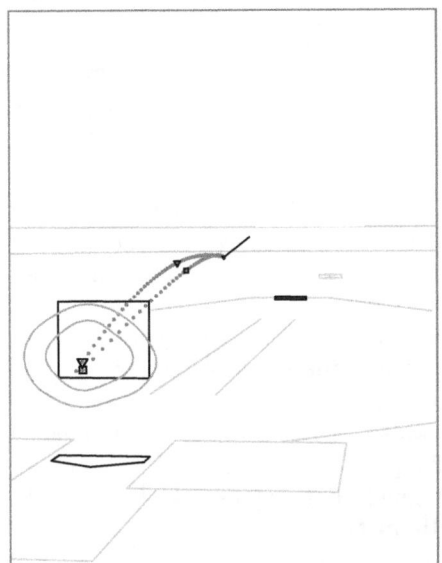

Pitch Shape vs RHH

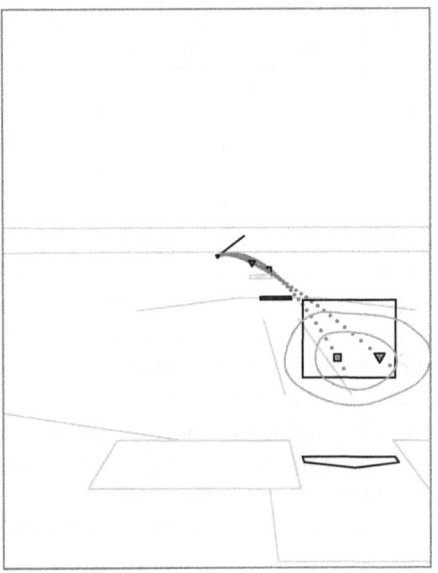

Type	Frequency	Velocity	H Movement	V Movement
● Fastball	9.1%	93 [101]	-13.9 [66]	-23.8 [76]
☐ Sinker	51.8%	91.3 [94]	-14.4 [90]	-35.9 [50]
▽ Slider	38.4%	76.7 [68]	15.4 [138]	-34.9 [97]

Michael Wacha RHP

Born: 07/01/91   Age: 30   Bats: R   Throws: R
Height: 6'6"   Weight: 215   Origin: Round 1, 2012 Draft (#19 overall)

YEAR	TEAM	LVL	AGE	W	L	SV	G	GS	IP	H	HR	BB/9	K/9	K	GB%	BABIP
2018	STL	MLB	26	8	2	0	15	15	84^1	68	9	3.8	7.6	71	44.7%	.253
2019	STL	MLB	27	6	7	0	29	24	126^2	143	26	3.9	7.4	104	48.0%	.318
2020	NYM	MLB	28	1	4	0	8	7	34	46	9	1.9	9.8	37	36.4%	.366
2021 FS	TB	MLB	29	9	8	0	26	26	150	142	20	3.2	8.4	140	43.8%	.292
2021 DC	TB	MLB	29	8	7	0	35	22	111	105	15	3.2	8.4	104	43.8%	.292

Comparables: Julio Teheran, Mat Latos, Jonathon Niese

No one expected Wacha's first year in Queens to be a replay of his high-water mark in 2017, but he may have dipped beneath even the low expectations that came with his one-year, $3 million contract. The righty was extremely hittable, with almost two-thirds of balls in play taking to the air, and many of them leaving the stadium. When he wasn't getting hit hard, he was suffering from shoulder inflammation that kept him from going deep into games and consigned him to the injured list for part of the season. There were a few encouraging signs in his peripherals—his walk rate was a career low, and his strikeout rate a career high—but hitters slugged .727 and .571 against his four-seamer and cutter, respectively. The Rays saw something they liked, though, and inked him to a repeat of his terms with the Mets.

YEAR	TEAM	LVL	AGE	WHIP	ERA	DRA-	WARP	MPH	FB%	WHF	CSP
2018	STL	MLB	26	1.23	3.20	89	1.3	96.0	43.0%	23.2%	
2019	STL	MLB	27	1.56	4.76	128	-0.7	95.4	50.8%	21.3%	
2020	NYM	MLB	28	1.56	6.62	99	0.3	95.9	42.5%	24.6%	
2021 FS	TB	MLB	29	1.31	4.03	92	2.1	95.7	47.3%	22.4%	46.8%
2021 DC	TB	MLB	29	1.31	4.03	92	1.5	95.7	47.3%	22.4%	46.8%

Michael Wacha, continued

Pitch Shape vs LHH

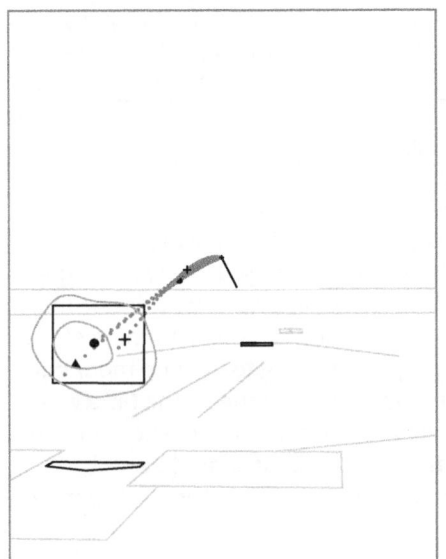

Pitch Shape vs RHH

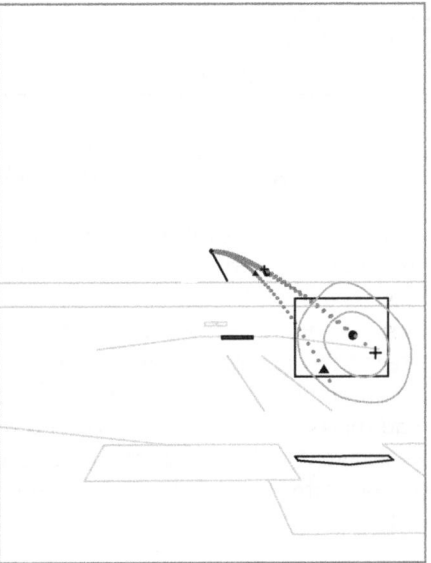

Type	Frequency	Velocity	H Movement	V Movement
● Fastball	42.5%	93.8 [104]	-7 [99]	-13.1 [106]
+ Cutter	27.1%	89 [104]	2.6 [104]	-24.5 [99]
▲ Changeup	29.2%	87 [107]	-12 [98]	-25.9 [104]

Ryan Yarbrough LHP

Born: 12/31/91 Age: 29 Bats: R Throws: L
Height: 6'5" Weight: 205 Origin: Round 4, 2014 Draft (#111 overall)

YEAR	TEAM	LVL	AGE	W	L	SV	G	GS	IP	H	HR	BB/9	K/9	K	GB%	BABIP
2018	TB	MLB	26	16	6	0	38	6	147^1	140	18	3.1	7.8	128	38.2%	.288
2019	DUR	AAA	27	2	1	0	5	4	26	24	2	1.0	12.1	35	42.4%	.344
2019	TB	MLB	27	11	6	0	28	14	141^2	121	15	1.3	7.4	117	42.8%	.264
2020	TB	MLB	28	1	4	0	11	9	55^2	54	5	1.9	7.1	44	40.9%	.299
2021 FS	TB	MLB	29	10	7	0	26	26	150	141	18	2.2	8.1	135	42.4%	.290
2021 DC	TB	MLB	29	9	7	0	36	24	125	117	15	2.2	8.1	112	42.4%	.290

Comparables: Steven Brault, Sean Manaea, Matt Strahm

    The soft-tossing Yarbrough was used as a starter in nine of his 11 appearances, setting a new career-high in start percentage. He rewarded the Rays—we'd like to think they'd consider it a reward, anyway—by working into the sixth inning or later in four of those games, including a seven-inning effort late in the year against the Orioles. Yarbrough isn't going to light up radar guns or contend for a Cy Young Award; what he should have done by the time you read this is offer one of the most interesting arbitration cases in recent memory, as his agent will have to attempt to explain why his client should be compensated as a starter despite more frequently being used as a reliever. Good luck.

YEAR	TEAM	LVL	AGE	WHIP	ERA	DRA-	WARP	MPH	FB%	WHF	CSP
2018	TB	MLB	26	1.29	3.91	107	0.3	91.0	63.7%	20.7%	
2019	DUR	AAA	27	1.04	3.81	58	1.0				
2019	TB	MLB	27	1.00	4.13	81	2.5	89.6	61.0%	22.3%	
2020	TB	MLB	28	1.19	3.56	97	0.6	88.7	59.4%	27.7%	
2021 FS	TB	MLB	29	1.19	3.64	85	2.7	89.7	61.2%	23.4%	49.2%
2021 DC	TB	MLB	29	1.19	3.64	85	2.0	89.7	61.2%	23.4%	49.2%

Ryan Yarbrough, continued

Pitch Shape vs LHH

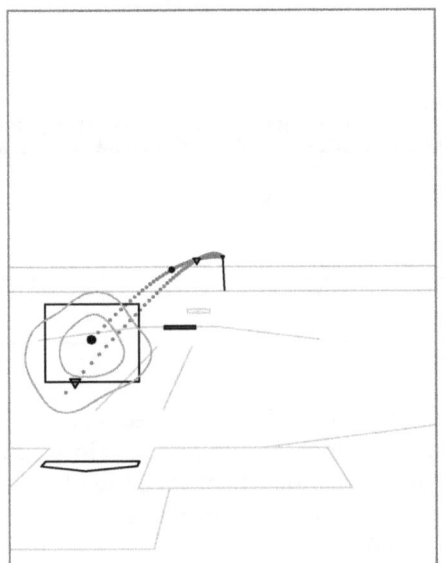

Pitch Shape vs RHH

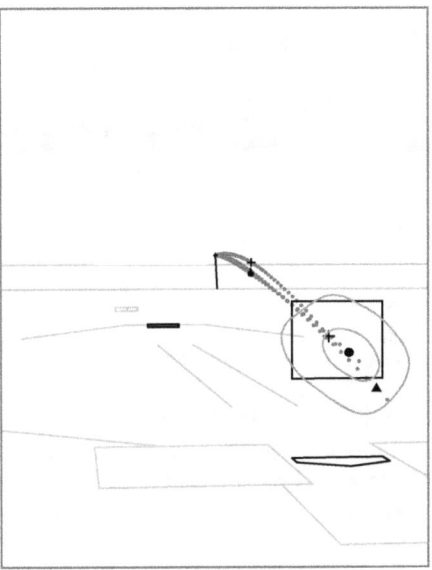

Type	Frequency	Velocity	H Movement	V Movement
● Fastball	23.2%	87.6 [84]	12.8 [71]	-21.7 [82]
+ Cutter	35.9%	83.2 [68]	-2.2 [102]	-28 [85]
▲ Changeup	29.8%	78.8 [75]	15 [82]	-34.4 [81]
▽ Slider	10.7%	71.1 [43]	-15.5 [139]	-46.1 [64]

PLAYER COMMENTS WITHOUT GRAPHS

Vidal Bruján 2B
Born: 02/09/98   Age: 23   Bats: S   Throws: R
Height: 5'10"   Weight: 180   Origin: International Free Agent, 2014

YEAR	TEAM	LVL	AGE	PA	R	2B	3B	HR	RBI	BB	K	SB	CS	AVG/OBP/SLG
2018	BG	LO-A	20	434	86	18	5	5	41	48	53	43	15	.313/.395/.427
2018	CHA	HI-A	20	114	26	7	2	4	12	15	15	12	4	.347/.434/.582
2019	CHA	HI-A	21	196	28	8	3	1	15	17	26	24	5	.290/.357/.386
2019	MTG	AA	21	233	28	9	4	3	25	20	35	24	8	.266/.336/.391
2021 FS	TB	MLB	23	600	66	25	5	10	62	44	110	27	12	.247/.310/.370
2021 DC	TB	MLB	23	33	3	1	0	0	3	2	6	1	1	.247/.310/.370

Comparables: Steve Lombardozzi, Corban Joseph, Jose Altuve

Hold with us for a sentence as we make a tenuous reference based on the spelling of two individuals' names. Ready? Here goes. According to the internet, the late author Gore Vidal once said that he died a little whenever a friend succeeded. Rays infield prospects like Mr. Brujan can probably relate. It's not enough that the Rays have Willy Adames and Brandon Lowe entrenched as their big-league double-play combination; they also have Wander Franco, Greg Jones, Xavier Edwards and other top-shelf youngsters jockeying for position on their organizational depth chart. That can make it difficult for anyone else to stand out. Brujan does, however, thanks to a pair of above-average tools (hit and speed). Lest any other Rays infielder feel gutted by our praise of Brujan, we'll end by noting that his defense is such that he could end up on the grass. See? Doesn't that make you feel a little better?

YEAR	TEAM	LVL	AGE	PA	DRC+	BABIP	BRR	FRAA	WARP
2018	BG	LO-A	20	434	140	.351	8.2	2B(87): 4.4	4.0
2018	CHA	HI-A	20	114	164	.380	1.0	2B(24): 4.5	1.4
2019	CHA	HI-A	21	196	131	.333	5.5	2B(29): 0.7, SS(14): 0.7	2.0
2019	MTG	AA	21	233	95	.304	-2.6	2B(33): 2.7, SS(15): -0.1	0.6
2021 FS	TB	MLB	23	600	86	.292	2.7	2B 4, SS 0	1.4
2021 DC	TB	MLB	23	33	86	.292	0.2	2B 0	0.1

Xavier Edwards SS

Born: 08/09/99 Age: 21 Bats: S Throws: R
Height: 5'10" Weight: 175 Origin: Round 1, 2018 Draft (#38 overall)

YEAR	TEAM	LVL	AGE	PA	R	2B	3B	HR	RBI	BB	K	SB	CS	AVG/OBP/SLG
2018	SD1	ROK	18	88	19	4	1	0	11	13	10	12	1	.384/.471/.466
2018	TRI	SS	18	107	21	4	0	0	5	18	15	10	0	.314/.438/.360
2019	FW	LO-A	19	344	44	13	4	1	30	30	35	20	9	.336/.392/.414
2019	LE	HI-A	19	217	32	5	4	0	13	14	19	14	2	.301/.349/.367
2021 FS	TB	MLB	21	600	53	25	3	6	52	45	114	20	7	.260/.319/.352

Comparables: José Ramírez, Jorge Polanco, Asdrúbal Cabrera

The dangers of the internet age—and especially the social media age—is that sometimes thoughts that should remain private are expressed publicly. Take, for instance, Blake Snell's raw reaction to the Tommy Pham trade. Snell, who was streaming on Twitch at the time, was dejected that the Rays would move one of their most productive hitters for—among other players—a "slapdick prospect." (Imagine explaining that sentence to Jim Leyland.) It was a funny moment, but it undersells Edwards' ability. He's a potential leadoff hitter, complete with plus bat-to-ball skills and elite speed, who has a chance to remain at shortstop. That's a good player, and one who will have an obvious Players' Weekend nickname once he reaches the Show.

YEAR	TEAM	LVL	AGE	PA	DRC+	BABIP	BRR	FRAA	WARP
2018	SD1	ROK	18	88		.438			
2018	TRI	SS	18	107	179	.380	-0.3	SS(19): -1.1, 2B(5): -0.0	0.7
2019	FW	LO-A	19	344	141	.371	0.2	2B(51): 4.1, SS(21): 3.1	3.4
2019	LE	HI-A	19	217	101	.331	3.5	2B(36): 0.2, SS(9): -1.2	0.9
2021 FS	TB	MLB	21	600	86	.318	1.5	2B 2, SS 1	1.2

Wander Franco SS

Born: 03/01/01   Age: 20   Bats: S   Throws: R
Height: 5'10"   Weight: 189   Origin: International Free Agent, 2017

YEAR	TEAM	LVL	AGE	PA	R	2B	3B	HR	RBI	BB	K	SB	CS	AVG/OBP/SLG
2018	PRN	ROK	17	273	46	10	7	11	57	27	19	4	3	.351/.418/.587
2019	BG	LO-A	18	272	42	16	5	6	29	30	20	14	9	.318/.390/.506
2019	CHA	HI-A	18	223	40	11	2	3	24	26	15	4	5	.339/.408/.464
2021 FS	TB	MLB	20	600	66	27	5	10	67	38	88	8	7	.264/.316/.390
2021 DC	TB	MLB	20	33	3	1	0	0	3	2	4	0	0	.264/.316/.390

Comparables: Jurickson Profar, Carlos Correa, Ronald Torreyes

Welcome to the 2021 edition of the *Baseball Prospectus Annual*. Wander Franco is still the game's top prospect. Had he played in a regular minor-league season in 2020, he would've likely posted above-average statistics despite being young for his league. He would've made dazzling plays at shortstop thanks to his strong arm and ample range, showed off a plus hit tool from both sides and tapped into his raw power enough to encourage. We would've been noting that, yup, all indications are Franco is a future superstar. Hopefully we'll get to see his talents in the majors once the Rays are done manipulating his service time.

YEAR	TEAM	LVL	AGE	PA	DRC+	BABIP	BRR	FRAA	WARP
2018	PRN	ROK	17	273		.346			
2019	BG	LO-A	18	272	158	.318	0.1	SS(53): -1.0	2.6
2019	CHA	HI-A	18	223	175	.346	4.3	SS(45): 8.1	3.9
2021 FS	TB	MLB	20	600	94	.299	0.8	SS 3	1.8
2021 DC	TB	MLB	20	33	94	.299	0.0	SS 0	0.1

Heriberto Hernandez C

Born: 12/16/99 Age: 21 Bats: R Throws: R
Height: 6'1" Weight: 180 Origin: International Free Agent, 2017

YEAR	TEAM	LVL	AGE	PA	R	2B	3B	HR	RBI	BB	K	SB	CS	AVG/OBP/SLG
2018	DSL RAN2	ROK	18	239	56	15	5	12	49	53	41	5	5	.292/.464/.635
2019	RAN	ROK	19	224	42	17	4	11	48	27	57	3	3	.344/.433/.646
2019	SPO	SS	19	10	4	0	0	0	1	2	3	3	0	.375/.500/.375
2021 FS	TB	MLB	21	600	46	21	3	7	47	48	211	6	4	.184/.257/.280

Comparables: Austin Meadows, Oswaldo Arcia, Joc Pederson

It's considered gauche to heap praise on first-base prospects barely out of rookie ball. It's okay in this case, because Hernandez can't really play first base, either; the Rangers moved him around between catcher, left, and first. While ordinarily that might be distracting, Hernandez never stopped hitting, which is probably all he'll be asked to do at the major league level. The Rangers gave him a spot on the alternate site despite his youth, and the limited nature of the practice probably didn't hurt him. To sum up, what you have is a youngster with huge offensive potential who offers very little by way of defense. The Rays will surely put his dynamic bat to use somehow following their acquisition of Hernandez in a deal for Nate Lowe.

YEAR	TEAM	LVL	AGE	PA	DRC+	BABIP	BRR	FRAA	WARP
2018	DSL RAN2	ROK	18	239		.315			
2019	RAN	ROK	19	224		.440			
2019	SPO	SS	19	10	163	.600	0.7	RF(1): -0.2	0.1
2021 FS	TB	MLB	21	600	49	.284	0.4	1B -1, C 0	-2.5

Ronaldo Hernández C

Born: 11/11/97 Age: 23 Bats: R Throws: R
Height: 6'1" Weight: 230 Origin: International Free Agent, 2014

YEAR	TEAM	LVL	AGE	PA	R	2B	3B	HR	RBI	BB	K	SB	CS	AVG/OBP/SLG
2018	BG	LO-A	20	449	68	20	1	21	79	31	69	10	4	.284/.339/.494
2019	CHA	HI-A	21	427	43	19	3	9	60	17	65	7	0	.265/.299/.397
2021 FS	TB	MLB	23	600	67	27	1	16	69	33	133	3	2	.240/.289/.381
2021 DC	TB	MLB	23	33	3	1	0	0	3	1	7	0	0	.240/.289/.381

Comparables: Travis d'Arnaud, Jesús Sucre, John Ryan Murphy

Hernandez has a strong arm behind the dish and plus power potential at it. The other aspects of his game need further refinement, which explains why he didn't appear in the majors despite being part of the Rays' 60-player pool and traveling with the taxi squad on a few road trips.

Tampa Bay Rays 2021

YEAR	TEAM	LVL	AGE	PA	DRC+	BABIP	BRR	FRAA	WARP
2018	BG	LO-A	20	449	132	.292	-0.8	C(85): 1.2	2.8
2019	CHA	HI-A	21	427	105	.290	1.8	C(81): 1.9	2.3
2021 FS	TB	MLB	23	600	85	.288	-0.6	C 0	1.3
2021 DC	TB	MLB	23	33	85	.288	0.0	C 0	0.1

Josh Lowe   CF
Born: 02/02/98   Age: 23   Bats: L   Throws: R
Height: 6'4"   Weight: 205   Origin: Round 1, 2016 Draft (#13 overall)

YEAR	TEAM	LVL	AGE	PA	R	2B	3B	HR	RBI	BB	K	SB	CS	AVG/OBP/SLG
2018	CHA	HI-A	20	455	62	25	3	6	47	47	117	18	6	.238/.322/.361
2019	MTG	AA	21	519	70	23	4	18	62	59	132	30	9	.252/.341/.442
2021 FS	TB	MLB	23	600	57	21	3	15	61	59	212	12	5	.206/.288/.346

Comparables: Michael Saunders, Luis Robert, Chris Young

This Lowe, Tampa Bay's top pick in 2016, should make his big-league debut in 2021. There are star-caliber tools here, but there's a good chance he's not going to hit enough against big-league pitching to make the most of them.

YEAR	TEAM	LVL	AGE	PA	DRC+	BABIP	BRR	FRAA	WARP
2018	CHA	HI-A	20	455	95	.318	1.1	CF(102): 4.1	0.8
2019	MTG	AA	21	519	128	.316	5.6	CF(110): -7.0, RF(9): 2.2, LF(1): -0.2	3.3
2021 FS	TB	MLB	23	600	74	.308	0.9	CF 4, RF 0	0.5

Francisco Mejía   C
Born: 10/27/95   Age: 25   Bats: S   Throws: R
Height: 5'8"   Weight: 188   Origin: International Free Agent, 2012

YEAR	TEAM	LVL	AGE	PA	R	2B	3B	HR	RBI	BB	K	SB	CS	AVG/OBP/SLG
2018	ELP	AAA	22	132	22	8	1	7	23	7	25	0	0	.328/.364/.582
2018	COL	AAA	22	336	32	22	1	7	45	18	58	0	0	.279/.328/.426
2018	SD	MLB	22	58	6	2	0	3	8	3	19	0	0	.185/.241/.389
2018	CLE	MLB	22	4	0	0	0	0	0	2	0	0	0	.000/.500/.000
2019	ELP	AAA	23	73	14	8	2	4	12	5	10	0	0	.365/.411/.746
2019	SD	MLB	23	244	27	11	2	8	22	13	56	1	1	.265/.316/.438
2020	SD	MLB	24	42	5	1	0	1	2	1	9	0	0	.077/.143/.179
2021 FS	TB	MLB	25	600	70	26	2	22	76	34	142	0	1	.244/.300/.422
2021 DC	TB	MLB	25	284	33	12	1	10	36	16	67	0	0	.244/.300/.422

Comparables: Tony Wolters, Randy Hundley, John Rabb

When the Padres first traded Brad Hand (and Adam Cimber) for Mejía, it looked like highway robbery. Trading a reliever a rebuilding team doesn't need in exchange for a premium catching prospect? That's a no-brainer. Now it looks like the Padres are fortunate it was a low-risk deal, because it appears that Cleveland received the better end of the trade. Hand has continued to excel while Mejía has struggled to gain traction. Even if you dismiss his horrid slash line as an aberration, he's struggled defensively to the extent that a position change would be justifiable. The problem is he hasn't hit well enough to play anywhere else. Mejía will enter 2021 with yet another shot at playing time in Tampa Bay, following the trade that sent Blake Snell to the Padres. He'll battle Mike Zunino for playing time out of the gate.

YEAR	TEAM	P. COUNT	FRM RUNS	BLK RUNS	THRW RUNS	TOT RUNS
2018	SD	1506	-0.7	-0.8	0.0	-1.5
2019	SD	7679	-0.8	0.1	-0.5	-1.2
2019	ELP	2100	1.9	0.0	0.0	1.9
2020	SD	1616	-0.4	-0.1	0.0	-0.5
2021	TB	10822	-1.6	-0.8	0.1	-2.3
2021	TB	10822	-1.6	0.3	0.1	-1.2

YEAR	TEAM	LVL	AGE	PA	DRC+	BABIP	BRR	FRAA	WARP
2018	ELP	AAA	22	132	121	.359	0.7	C(26): 1.3	0.9
2018	COL	AAA	22	336	101	.321	-1.2	C(41): 4.6, LF(22): -3.2, RF(7): -1.0	0.7
2018	SD	MLB	22	58	72	.219	0.2	C(10): -1.7	-0.1
2018	CLE	MLB	22	4	69	.000			0.0
2019	ELP	AAA	23	73	136	.365	-1.0	C(16): 2.6	0.8
2019	SD	MLB	23	244	90	.319	2.0	C(60): -0.6, LF(4): 0.3	1.0
2020	SD	MLB	24	42	79	.069	0.4	C(16): 0.3	0.1
2021 FS	TB	MLB	25	600	94	.291	-0.7	C -3, LF 0	1.5
2021 DC	TB	MLB	25	284	94	.291	-0.3	C -2	0.7

Chris Archer RHP

Born: 09/26/88 Age: 32 Bats: R Throws: R
Height: 6'2" Weight: 195 Origin: Round 5, 2006 Draft (#161 overall)

YEAR	TEAM	LVL	AGE	W	L	SV	G	GS	IP	H	HR	BB/9	K/9	K	GB%	BABIP
2018	TB	MLB	29	3	5	0	17	17	96	102	11	2.9	9.6	102	45.3%	.343
2018	PIT	MLB	29	3	3	0	10	10	52^1	53	8	3.1	10.3	60	45.5%	.331
2019	PIT	MLB	30	3	9	0	23	23	119^2	114	25	4.1	10.8	143	35.2%	.304
2021 FS	TB	MLB	32	9	8	0	26	26	150	135	24	3.5	10.1	168	40.2%	.292
2021 DC	TB	MLB	32	7	6	0	22	22	111	100	18	3.5	10.1	124	40.2%	.292

Comparables: Sonny Gray, Zack Wheeler, Gio González

Proof that life does not give us what we deserve, the affable Archer's tenure in Pittsburgh took another disastrous turn when he was diagnosed with Thoracic Outlet Syndrome in June, ruling him out for the season. TOS isn't as predictable a recovery process as Tommy John, but promising data is emerging as the procedure becomes more common and therefore more studied. As a pitcher who relies more on mixing his secondaries and his swing-and-miss slider rather than overpowering velocity, which can be affected by TOS surgery, he's a good candidate to bounce back from this condition. However, while it's likely Archer will return to the mound, it's almost certain he'll do it wearing a different cap, as the always unstinting Bob Nutting made the agonizing choice of paying him $250,000 rather than $11 million for his option.

YEAR	TEAM	LVL	AGE	WHIP	ERA	DRA-	WARP	MPH	FB%	WHF	CSP
2018	TB	MLB	29	1.39	4.31	92	1.3	96.5	45.6%	29.1%	
2018	PIT	MLB	29	1.36	4.30	96	0.6	96.7	49.3%	28.1%	
2019	PIT	MLB	30	1.41	5.19	90	1.8	96.0	50.5%	29.7%	
2021 FS	TB	MLB	32	1.30	4.12	94	1.9	96.2	49.1%	29.4%	46.2%
2021 DC	TB	MLB	32	1.30	4.12	94	1.4	96.2	49.1%	29.4%	46.2%

Shane Baz RHP
Born: 06/17/99   Age: 22   Bats: R   Throws: R
Height: 6'2"   Weight: 190   Origin: Round 1, 2017 Draft (#12 overall)

YEAR	TEAM	LVL	AGE	W	L	SV	G	GS	IP	H	HR	BB/9	K/9	K	GB%	BABIP
2018	PRN	ROK	19	0	2	0	2	2	7	11	1	7.7	6.4	5	48.0%	.417
2018	BRS	ROK	19	4	3	0	10	10	45^1	45	2	4.6	10.7	54	63.0%	.344
2019	BG	LO-A	20	3	2	0	17	17	81^1	63	5	4.1	9.6	87	37.1%	.280
2021 FS	TB	MLB	22	2	3	0	57	0	50	47	8	6.1	8.1	45	41.4%	.279

Comparables: Casey Crosby, Daniel Norris, Elvin Ramirez

Baz, the third piece of the Chris Archer return, tends to get overlooked in the deal's accounting because he hasn't yet made his big-league debut. That'll change soon enough. Baz has a high-quality fastball-slider combination that enables him to miss bats and evade barrels (he's yielded 10 homers in 157 professional innings). He's also a good athlete who has exhibited enough knowhow on the mound to like his chances of making future adjustments. Baz still needs to develop his changeup and his command, of course, but there's reason to believe he could make an already bad trade look even worse.

YEAR	TEAM	LVL	AGE	WHIP	ERA	DRA-	WARP	MPH	FB%	WHF	CSP
2018	PRN	ROK	19	2.43	7.71						
2018	BRS	ROK	19	1.50	3.97						
2019	BG	LO-A	20	1.23	2.99	79	1.2				
2021 FS	TB	MLB	22	1.62	5.52	119	-0.3				

Nick Bitsko RHP
Born: 06/16/02   Age: 19   Bats: R   Throws: R
Height: 6'4"   Weight: 225   Origin: Round 1, 2020 Draft (#24 overall)

The idea that Bitsko was drafted based solely on some videos posted on the internet is a reach: he was *also* drafted because his name sounds like a three-year-old trying to read the branding on a package of Oreos. Either way, he was considered one of the top prospects in the 2021 class before he reclassified to 2020. The pandemic did cost teams valuable in-person looks at Bitsko, but that didn't prevent the Rays from selecting him at No. 24 based on the promise of his prototypical size and stuff. It remains to be seen if offseason shoulder surgery will threaten that promise in the short term.

Brent Honeywell Jr. RHP
Born: 03/31/95 Age: 26 Bats: R Throws: R
Height: 6'2" Weight: 195 Origin: Round 2, 2014 Draft (#72 overall)

YEAR	TEAM	LVL	AGE	W	L	SV	G	GS	IP	H	HR	BB/9	K/9	K	GB%	BABIP
2021 FS	TB	MLB	26	10	7	0	26	26	150	131	22	2.9	9.4	157	34.6%	.281
2021 DC	TB	MLB	26	2	2	0	12	6	30.3	26	4	2.9	9.4	31	34.6%	.281

Comparables: Mitch Keller, Zack Littell, Stephen Gonsalves

Honeywell hasn't thrown a pitch in a professional game in over three years. The hope, once again, is that he will resume his career this coming season, though he's coming off his fourth elbow surgery in that time. Give Honeywell this much: he contributed to the Rays' playoff run in his own special way, by which we mean he allowed Randy Arozarena to wear his cowboy boots. "I call them the power boots," Arozarena told MLB.com's Juan Toribio. "My teammates started telling me that those were the boots that were giving me good luck." Now, if only some of that good luck would stick to Honeywell…

YEAR	TEAM	LVL	AGE	WHIP	ERA	DRA-	WARP	MPH	FB%	WHF	CSP
2021 FS	TB	MLB	26	1.20	3.60	87	2.5				
2021 DC	TB	MLB	26	1.20	3.60	87	0.5				

Andrew Kittredge RHP
Born: 03/17/90 Age: 31 Bats: R Throws: R
Height: 6'1" Weight: 230 Origin: Round 45, 2008 Draft (#1360 overall)

YEAR	TEAM	LVL	AGE	W	L	SV	G	GS	IP	H	HR	BB/9	K/9	K	GB%	BABIP
2018	DUR	AAA	28	6	0	2	21	1	46	41	3	2.3	11.3	58	39.0%	.317
2018	TB	MLB	28	3	2	0	33	3	38[1]	54	7	4.0	7.0	30	49.6%	.376
2019	DUR	AAA	29	2	1	6	27	1	37[1]	24	3	1.4	13.3	55	49.4%	.280
2019	TB	MLB	29	1	0	0	37	7	49[2]	51	7	2.2	10.5	58	50.0%	.336
2020	TB	MLB	30	0	0	1	8	1	8	8	0	2.2	3.4	3	57.7%	.308
2021 FS	TB	MLB	31	2	2	0	57	0	50	45	6	2.5	9.3	51	47.2%	.296
2021 DC	TB	MLB	31	1	1	0	25	0	33	30	4	2.5	9.3	34	47.2%	.296

Comparables: Paul Sewald, Evan Marshall, Jacob Barnes

Baseball can be such a cruel game sometimes. Kittredge earned a save on Monday, August 11, and then served as an opener the next night. Five pitches into that "start," he departed with a torn UCL. If he's lucky, and if he heals quickly, his next big-league outing should come late in the 2021 season.

YEAR	TEAM	LVL	AGE	WHIP	ERA	DRA-	WARP	MPH	FB%	WHF	CSP
2018	DUR	AAA	28	1.15	2.74	50	1.4				
2018	TB	MLB	28	1.85	7.75	135	-0.5	94.8	39.9%	22.5%	
2019	DUR	AAA	29	0.80	1.93	27	1.8				
2019	TB	MLB	29	1.27	4.17	76	0.9	96.3	58.1%	31.5%	
2020	TB	MLB	30	1.25	2.25	100	0.1	95.9	47.8%	15.0%	
2021 FS	TB	MLB	31	1.20	3.49	83	0.7	95.9	52.3%	27.2%	46.5%
2021 DC	TB	MLB	31	1.20	3.49	83	0.5	95.9	52.3%	27.2%	46.5%

Shane McClanahan LHP

Born: 04/28/97   Age: 24   Bats: L   Throws: L
Height: 6'1"   Weight: 200   Origin: Round 1, 2018 Draft (#31 overall)

YEAR	TEAM	LVL	AGE	W	L	SV	G	GS	IP	H	HR	BB/9	K/9	K	GB%	BABIP
2018	PRN	ROK	21	0	0	0	2	2	4	2	0	2.2	15.8	7	50.0%	.333
2018	RAY	ROK	21	0	0	0	2	2	3	1	0	0.0	18.0	6	50.0%	.250
2019	BG	LO-A	22	4	4	0	11	10	53	38	3	5.3	12.6	74	47.5%	.304
2019	CHA	HI-A	22	6	1	0	9	8	49^1	33	1	1.5	10.8	59	40.7%	.267
2019	MTG	AA	22	1	1	0	4	4	18^1	30	3	2.9	10.3	21	39.7%	.450
2021 FS	TB	MLB	24	9	9	0	26	26	150	137	23	4.8	9.3	155	40.5%	.288
2021 DC	TB	MLB	24	3	3	0	28	4	41.7	38	6	4.8	9.3	43	40.5%	.288

Comparables: Julio Urías, Brendan McKay, Austin Voth

McClanahan became the first pitcher in history to make his major-league debut in the postseason. He was used in a low-leverage role, but showed high-leverage stuff: a fastball that touched triple digits, and a slider that sat near 90 mph. His initial introduction to the majors didn't go too hot otherwise—he tossed four innings in the playoffs, surrendering five runs on eight hits and two walks—but he'll likely return to starting in the minors in 2021. Don't be surprised if he ends up pitching meaningful innings for the Rays again this fall, either as a starter or as a late-inning reliever.

YEAR	TEAM	LVL	AGE	WHIP	ERA	DRA-	WARP	MPH	FB%	WHF	CSP
2018	PRN	ROK	21	0.75	0.00						
2018	RAY	ROK	21	0.33	0.00						
2019	BG	LO-A	22	1.30	3.40	78	0.8				
2019	CHA	HI-A	22	0.83	1.46	51	1.5				
2019	MTG	AA	22	1.96	8.35	163	-0.7				
2021 FS	TB	MLB	24	1.45	4.65	106	0.9				
2021 DC	TB	MLB	24	1.45	4.65	106	0.2				

Brendan McKay LHP

Born: 12/18/95   Age: 25   Bats: L   Throws: L
Height: 6'2"   Weight: 220   Origin: Round 1, 2017 Draft (#4 overall)

YEAR	TEAM	LVL	AGE	W	L	SV	G	GS	IP	H	HR	BB/9	K/9	K	GB%	BABIP
2018	RAY	ROK	22	0	0	0	2	2	6	2	0	1.5	13.5	9	58.3%	.167
2018	BG	LO-A	22	2	0	0	6	6	24²	8	1	0.7	14.6	40	60.5%	.167
2018	CHA	HI-A	22	3	2	0	11	9	47²	45	2	2.1	10.2	54	36.8%	.355
2019	MTG	AA	23	3	0	0	8	7	41²	25	2	1.9	13.4	62	40.5%	.280
2019	DUR	AAA	23	3	0	0	7	6	32	17	1	2.5	11.2	40	45.1%	.232
2019	TB	MLB	23	2	4	0	13	11	49	53	8	2.9	10.3	56	35.4%	.333
2021 FS	TB	MLB	25	10	7	0	26	26	150	130	22	3.0	10.5	175	39.9%	.292
2021 DC	TB	MLB	25	2	2	0	16	6	33	28	4	3.0	10.5	38	39.9%	.292

Comparables: Nick Margevicius, Eric Lauer, Tarik Skubal

McKay entered the spring ranked as one of the consensus 30 or so best prospects in the game: BP had him at 28. It was all downhill from there—and not in the good, easy-breezy sense. McKay had one of the organization's toughest summers, beginning with a positive COVID-19 test. Soon after his return, he was shut down with a sore throwing shoulder, which eventually necessitated surgery. Ruh roh. With all his polish and his theoretical two-way ability (he hasn't really hit in a few years), McKay was supposed to be one of the safer pitching prospects in the game. Let his 2020 be a reminder that there is no such thing.

YEAR	TEAM	LVL	AGE	WHIP	ERA	DRA-	WARP	MPH	FB%	WHF	CSP
2018	RAY	ROK	22	0.50	1.50						
2018	BG	LO-A	22	0.41	1.09	56	0.8				
2018	CHA	HI-A	22	1.17	3.21	62	1.2				
2019	MTG	AA	23	0.82	1.30	51	1.2				
2019	DUR	AAA	23	0.81	0.84	31	1.6				
2019	TB	MLB	23	1.41	5.14	118	0.0	95.4	70.0%	23.8%	
2021 FS	TB	MLB	25	1.20	3.58	84	2.8	95.4	70.0%	23.8%	50.1%
2021 DC	TB	MLB	25	1.20	3.58	84	0.6	95.4	70.0%	23.8%	50.1%

Colin Poche LHP

Born: 01/17/94 Age: 27 Bats: L Throws: L
Height: 6'3" Weight: 225 Origin: Round 14, 2016 Draft (#419 overall)

YEAR	TEAM	LVL	AGE	W	L	SV	G	GS	IP	H	HR	BB/9	K/9	K	GB%	BABIP
2018	MTG	AA	24	1	0	0	3	0	5	1	0	0.0	16.2	9	28.6%	.143
2018	JXN	AA	24	0	0	1	9	0	11	3	0	1.6	18.8	23	0.0%	.250
2018	DUR	AAA	24	5	0	1	28	2	50	29	2	3.1	14.0	78	25.8%	.300
2019	DUR	AAA	25	2	2	0	20	2	27^1	32	4	3.0	15.8	48	35.4%	.459
2019	TB	MLB	25	5	5	2	51	0	51^2	33	9	3.3	12.5	72	18.0%	.238
2021 FS	TB	MLB	27	3	2	0	57	0	50	36	8	3.2	12.4	68	27.4%	.270
2021 DC	TB	MLB	27	0	0	0	12	0	13	9	2	3.2	12.4	18	27.4%	.270

Comparables: Aaron Bummer, A.J. Minter, Phil Maton

Poche is one of the most monomaniacal pitchers in the majors. He threw 769 very nice regular-season fastballs in 2019, as opposed to just 100 non-fastballs. Alas, Poche's elbow popped before he could throw any kind of pitch in 2020, resulting in a year lost to Tommy John surgery.

YEAR	TEAM	LVL	AGE	WHIP	ERA	DRA-	WARP	MPH	FB%	WHF	CSP
2018	MTG	AA	24	0.20	0.00	49	0.2				
2018	JXN	AA	24	0.45	0.00	11	0.6				
2018	DUR	AAA	24	0.92	1.08	61	1.2				
2019	DUR	AAA	25	1.50	6.26	74	0.7				
2019	TB	MLB	25	1.01	4.70	88	0.6	95.0	88.5%	35.1%	
2021 FS	TB	MLB	27	1.09	3.07	73	1.0	95.0	88.5%	35.1%	50.1%
2021 DC	TB	MLB	27	1.09	3.07	73	0.3	95.0	88.5%	35.1%	50.1%

Chaz Roe RHP

Born: 10/09/86 Age: 34 Bats: R Throws: R
Height: 6'5" Weight: 190 Origin: Round 1, 2005 Draft (#32 overall)

YEAR	TEAM	LVL	AGE	W	L	SV	G	GS	IP	H	HR	BB/9	K/9	K	GB%	BABIP
2018	TB	MLB	31	1	3	1	61	0	50^1	35	6	2.9	9.5	53	46.8%	.244
2019	TB	MLB	32	1	3	1	71	0	51	49	3	5.5	11.5	65	43.2%	.359
2020	TB	MLB	33	2	0	1	10	0	9^1	10	0	2.9	8.7	9	26.9%	.385
2021 FS	TB	MLB	34	2	2	0	57	0	50	45	6	3.8	9.7	53	43.5%	.297
2021 DC	TB	MLB	34	2	2	0	45	0	39.3	35	4	3.8	9.7	42	43.5%	.297

Comparables: Steve Cishek, Brad Brach, Tyler Clippard

If you're hungry for Roe's signature slider, you'll have to wait until his kitchen reopens sometime in 2021. He was shut down after 10 appearances because he felt discomfort in his arm that was later discovered to be unrelated to ligament damage. Roe is a season away from reaching free agency, so here's hoping he can make a full recovery and cash in next winter on several years of solid relief work.

YEAR	TEAM	LVL	AGE	WHIP	ERA	DRA-	WARP	MPH	FB%	WHF	CSP
2018	TB	MLB	31	1.01	3.58	82	0.7	93.8	47.4%	26.6%	
2019	TB	MLB	32	1.57	4.06	93	0.4	93.3	28.9%	27.8%	
2020	TB	MLB	33	1.39	2.89	104	0.1	92.7	25.8%	22.1%	
2021 FS	TB	MLB	34	1.33	4.02	91	0.5	93.3	33.0%	26.6%	48.6%
2021 DC	TB	MLB	34	1.33	4.02	91	0.4	93.3	33.0%	26.6%	48.6%

Joe Ryan RHP

Born: 06/05/96 Age: 25 Bats: R Throws: R
Height: 6'2" Weight: 205 Origin: Round 7, 2018 Draft (#210 overall)

YEAR	TEAM	LVL	AGE	W	L	SV	G	GS	IP	H	HR	BB/9	K/9	K	GB%	BABIP
2018	HV	SS	22	2	1	0	12	7	36^1	26	3	3.5	12.6	51	35.4%	.303
2019	BG	LO-A	23	2	2	0	6	6	27^2	19	2	3.6	15.3	47	28.6%	.315
2019	CHA	HI-A	23	7	2	0	15	13	82^2	47	3	1.3	12.2	112	36.6%	.246
2019	MTG	AA	23	0	0	0	3	3	13^1	11	2	2.7	16.2	24	23.1%	.375
2021 FS	TB	MLB	25	9	8	0	26	26	150	125	22	3.7	10.9	181	35.9%	.286

Comparables: Alex Reyes, Drew Rasmussen, Brad Mills

Ryan has struck out more than 13 batters per nine so far in his professional career despite relying on his fastball to an unseemly degree. Provided he keeps missing bats like he has, he could end up playing the Josh Fleming role for the Rays in 2021.

YEAR	TEAM	LVL	AGE	WHIP	ERA	DRA-	WARP	MPH	FB%	WHF	CSP
2018	HV	SS	22	1.10	3.72	47	1.3				
2019	BG	LO-A	23	1.08	2.93	59	0.7				
2019	CHA	HI-A	23	0.71	1.42	41	3.0				
2019	MTG	AA	23	1.12	3.38	85	0.1				
2021 FS	TB	MLB	25	1.25	3.85	91	2.2				

Cole Wilcox   RHP
Born: 07/14/99   Age: 21   Bats: R   Throws: R
Height: 6'5"   Weight: 232   Origin: Round 3, 2020 Draft (#80 overall)

The Padres may have drafted Wilcox in the third round, but they paid him like a first-rounder, ponying up more than $3 million so that he'd go pro. Wilcox has the raw stuff and the potential to make the investment look sound, though his command could ultimately force him into relief. He was a part of the four-player package San Diego used to acquire Blake Snell in the offseason.

Rays Prospects

The State of the System:
Comparing farm systems across eras is incredibly tricky, but if you told me this was the deepest collection of prospect talent ever, I'd be inclined to believe you.

The Top Ten:

1. ★ ★ ★ 2021 Top 101 Prospect #1 ★ ★ ★

Wander Franco SS   OFP: 70   ETA: 2021, as needed
Born: 03/01/01   Age: 20   Bats: S   Throws: R   Height: 5'10"   Weight: 189
Origin: International Free Agent, 2017

The Report: What more is there really to say about the best prospect in baseball? Franco is a potentially elite hitter, who should regularly hit .300 and post high OBPs due to one of the most advanced approaches you'll see in a teenaged hitter—yes he's still a teenager until March. The raw power is plus, but may play higher in games due to the sheer volume of quality contact. The left-handed swing is ahead of the right-handed one in terms of both hit and power, but that's not uncommon for a switch-hitter of his age, and that should smooth out with more reps against quality southpaws. Franco is an above-average runner for now, but has a blocky physique, and I'd expect the speed to play more in the average range by the time he's in his mid-20s. He's a solid infielder, rangey with smooth actions, but everything might fit a little better at second base than shortstop, and he's prone to the occasional young infielder hiccup.

Development Track: Franco played at the alternate site and even made the playoff taxi squad—you might have caught him on the field in a cutoff T-shirt showing off some bigger arms while celebrating the Rays' ALCS win. He then went to the Dominican Winter League for a bit, before a sore bicep caused him to be shut down. It sounds fairly minor, so expect Franco to be in the major league mix as soon as the Rays want to start his service time clock in 2021.

Variance: Low. You could argue because of the positional value and merely plus power that there are a small handful of prospects with a better 90th percentile outcome than Franco. He's the most likely to be at least a good regular for a decade though.

Mark Barry's Fantasy Take: So many things are different in the world since the last time we put out a Rays list. One thing not different: Wander Franco. He's the best prospect in the system, the best prospect in baseball, and probably a top-30 overall dynasty option.

─────── ★ ★ ★ *2021 Top 101 Prospect* **#20** ★ ★ ★ ───────

2 Randy Arozarena LF   OFP: 60   ETA: Debuted in 2019
Born: 02/28/95   Age: 26   Bats: R   Throws: R   Height: 5'11"   Weight: 185
Origin: International Free Agent, 2016

The Report: It's entirely possible Arozarena started his breakout at the end of 2019. Long more of a hit-over-power, speedy, maybe tweener type as a prospect, he popped 12 home runs in 64 games with the Triple-A Memphis Redbirds. But that's the Pacific Coast League with the MLB rabbit ball. Whenever it happened, the power breakout is real. It might be 30+ home run power, as Arozarena sure looks like he has the loft and strength now to have plus-plus game power. Even if the aggressive approach—especially against same-side breaking stuff—limits him to an average hit tool, and 20 or so home runs, his speed will make him an average center fielder and he'd be plus in a corner. That's a solid regular, and if you watched him in the playoffs, it's pretty clear there's star upside.

Development Track: Arozarena is only eligible because of the vagaries of the shortened season. He's clearly a present above-average major leaguer and will be an every day outfielder for the 2021 Rays. Arozarena was detained in Mexico in November after domestic violence allegations. His ex-partner declined to press charges.

Variance: Medium. We've seen him make adjustments against major-league breaking stuff as he's gone along, but there's still some hit tool risk. Conversely, if the late-season and playoff performance is real, he's an All-Star.

Mark Barry's Fantasy Take: Arozarena is one of the harder dudes to project heading into 2021, and I wish I knew whether he'd been stuck in a room doing push ups and eating chicken since the World Series. He's likely to hit some homers and steal some bases, and his ultimate fantasy upside will rest with whether he can trim some whiffs from his K-rate, to boost his batting average. His value is already sky high, so while it would be nice to see more, I'm not sure you'll have the chance before making an acquisition.

─────── ★ ★ ★ *2021 Top 101 Prospect* **#24** ★ ★ ★ ───────

3 Shane Baz RHP   OFP: 60   ETA: 2022
Born: 06/17/99   Age: 22   Bats: R   Throws: R   Height: 6'2"   Weight: 190
Origin: Round 1, 2017 Draft (#12 overall)

The Report: The third piece in the Chris Archer deal is the only one with prospect eligibility left, and he's a hell of a pitching prospect. Baz has easy plus-plus cheese, sitting in the upper-90s and routinely hitting 100. He pairs the fastball with a plus power slider with good tilt. The change-up flashes but is a work in progres. Although as you might have noted with another pitcher in that trade—Tyler Glasnow—when your top two pitches are this good, you don't need to throw your third one all that much. However, also like Glasnow, Baz can struggle with his command and control at times. It's not quite as effectively wild as Glasnow was as a prospect, but both the command and control are below average and that will need to be ironed out to cement him as a starting pitcher, well as much as the Rays use a traditional starter anyway.

Development Track: Baz has spent all of 80 innings above short-season ball so far. The alternate site work might allow him to start 2021 in Double-A, but he could use a full, normalish, minor league season to really put a stamp on where he is as a pitching prospect right now. The stuff isn't a question, what role it's best utilized in is.

Variance: Medium. Baz may need to tone down the "grip it and rip it" mechanics a little, but he can give back some of the top-end velocity for command and still have plenty of stuff. Of course that trade off can be easier said than done. So relief risk remains.

Mark Barry's Fantasy Take: The Rays of It All does throw a wrench into evaluating a lot of their arms in terms of fantasy. Sure, Glasnow is given a little leash, but many of their starters don't venture into the waters of the dreaded third time through the order. That's fine, it just caps the fantasy ceiling. For Baz, he has definitely displayed a knack for striking dudes out, but I worry he won't be trusted with a ton of volume. I also worry that's a sentiment that will be shared with most Rays pitching prospects.

4

Luis Patiño   RHP   OFP: 60   ETA: Debuted in 2020
Born: 10/26/99   Age: 21   Bats: R   Throws: R   Height: 6'1"   Weight: 192
Origin: International Free Agent, 2016

The Report: We are four prospects into this list now and we still can't manage worse than "one of the best pitching prospects in baseball" as an epithet. Patiño projects for four above-average pitches, and not in that "squint to get them to 55" way either. The fastball sits mid-90s with explosive life as a starter, and he can find more velocity when he needs it. The slider is a plus pitch, a power mid-80s breaker that can also show as a 70 grade offering when there's more bottom to it. The curve isn't a mere second breaking ball look, but an above-average offering in its own right with hard, late 11-5 action. The change can be on the firm side, but projects as a potential third plus pitch due to the tumble and fade it can flash. Patiño is on the smaller side, and while he's smoothed out the delivery some as a pro, there's still a big leg kick and he throws across his body some, which can impact his command and control.

Development Track: Patiño was called up to the majors from the alternate site in August to try and bolster a leaky Padres 'pen. He was making the jump to the bis after just a brief Double-A cup of coffee and asked to pitch in a new role on the fly. There were some growing pains, and Patiño struggled badly with his command and control. However, the 20-year-old's stuff looked lively and he missed plenty of major-league bats among his struggles. We do think his 2020 was a slight negative for the overall profile projection, but that's almost all "well, we think the reliever risk is a bit higher until we see command improvements." It's more than a minor quibble, but we aren't all that worried about him.

Variance: Medium. The stuff will play in the majors, the command will determine when, where, and how well. FWIW, If you were going to acquire a high end pitching prospect to use in a similar manner to how the Rays used Snell in order to maximize his in-game impact, Patiño would be among the pitching prospects I think could benefit most from that 30-start, 150-inning type workload.

Mark Barry's Fantasy Take: I like Patiño a little bit more than Baz, personally. I think he carries more strikeout upside and a better chance at logging innings. He also walks a bunch of guys, but I guess nobody's perfect. Also, depending on what the Rays do in terms of service-time manipulation, Patiño could be impactful as quickly as this season.

────── ★ ★ ★ *2021 Top 101 Prospect* **#67** ★ ★ ★ ──────

5   **Vidal Bruján   2B**   OFP: 60   ETA: 2021, as needed
Born: 02/09/98   Age: 23   Bats: S   Throws: R   Height: 5'10"   Weight: 180
Origin: International Free Agent, 2014

The Report: Bruján's profile is carried by a plus hit tool and plus-plus speed. The swing is contact-oriented with minimal over-the-fence power, but don't mistake it for slappy, as Bruján has strong wrists that generate plus bat speed from both sides. He can drive the ball into the gaps, which should allow him to run into plenty of doubles and triples, even if the home run pop remains in the single digits. The approach can tend to the aggressive side, but he'll take a walk if given it. The bat is going to be batting-average dependent, but those averages could start with a 3 some years. Defensively, Bruján has split time at the middle infield spits, but is a much better fit for second base as the arm is merely above-average and the hands and actions don't pop quite enough for the 6. His best actual defensive fit might be center field, and he did play there a couple times in the 2019 Arizona Fall League. Bruján could use the defensive flexibility regardless, and the path to middle infield playing time in the Trop is pretty well blocked at the moment.

Development Track: Bruján spent time at the alternate site, the Rays' playoff taxi squad, and then the Dominican Winter League. As 2020 developmental opportunities go, that's not a bad amount of reps. Bruján didn't dominate

Double-A the first time of asking in 2019, but assuming some consolidation time in the upper minors in 2021, should be ready for a major league opportunity if and when a spot opens up in Tampa.

Variance: Medium. Bruján can hit a little, run a bunch, and at least stand at all three up-the-middle spots. At worst that's a good 450 PA bench piece, but I think the actual delta here is fairly low and clustered around "solid regular."

Mark Barry's Fantasy Take: He's got LEGS and he knows how to use them—you know, for steals and such. Bruján makes a ton of contact, which I personally adore, and does so with plus speed. His stolen base efficiency has been improving as well, which certainly bodes well for his future green light. There's probably not any power coming, but that's OK. The potential for sweet, sweet steals is enough to keep him in the top-40 for dynasty prospects.

6 — 2021 Top 101 Prospect #80

Shane McClanahan LHP   OFP: 60   ETA: Debuted in 2020, sorta
Born: 04/28/97   Age: 24   Bats: L   Throws: L   Height: 6'1"   Weight: 200
Origin: Round 1, 2018 Draft (#31 overall)

The Report: McClanahan's fastball is absolutely electric. He sits in the high-90s and hit 100 mph in the playoffs. It's difficult to pick up and it moves around; it's just a tough pitch for batters to deal with. He pairs that with a slurvy low-to-mid-80s breaking ball. It's a knee-buckler when it's right, but he struggles to throw it with consistency and command. We also think it's pretty likely that he's going to end up in the bullpen; our staff opinions on this range from "there's an outside chance he'll start" to "there's very little chance he'll start." His changeup is underdeveloped (he barely threw it in his playoff cameo), his command isn't great, and his delivery is inconsistent. These are all major relief markers.

Development Track: McClanahan was called up for the postseason, and indeed became the first pitcher in major-league history to make his debut in the playoffs, where he pitched low-to-low-medium leverage innings for the Rays on their pennant run. His stuff was nasty and his command was all over the place, so he basically pitched to his report.

Variance: Medium. It's a really good fastball, but our confidence in him ever making 30 starts is low.

Mark Barry's Fantasy Take: I think the Rays tipped their hand for McLanahan's usage pattern, calling on him to make four appearances from the bullpen. Best case scenario, he winds up as a 2+ inning guy or part of the Rays Famous Closer Carousel. Worst case scenario, he winds up as an overqualified version of whatever the modern-day equivalent of a LOOGY is.

★ ★ ★ *2021 Top 101 Prospect* **#93** ★ ★ ★

7 Xavier Edwards SS — OFP: 60 — ETA: Late 2021/Early 2022
Born: 08/09/99 — Age: 21 — Bats: S — Throws: R — Height: 5'10" — Weight: 175
Origin: Round 1, 2018 Draft (#38 overall)

The Report: We talk a lot about whether prospects have carrying tools. Edwards has two. His hit tool has received a consistent plus evaluation in our live looks, between his quick hands, his strong bat-to-ball ability, and his excellent plate approach. He's also lightning fast, with 80 grade speed, 70 on his worst days. So it's not hard to come up with the contours of a very good player here, driven by averages around .300 and a ton of speed, mixed in with some defensive versatility. But there's major flaws too. Edwards has basically no present game power—he's hit just one homer in 168 professional games—and he doesn't project to pick a whole lot up later on. We're naturally wary of hit tool projections that are backed up by so little power and haven't been shown to work at the highest levels. His arm probably isn't strong enough for shortstop, so his positional versatility might end up just being second and the outfield (where we assume his speed would play up).

Development Track: Edwards was traded to the Rays last offseason. The team brought him to the alternate site mid-season, and his batted ball data there was exactly as weak as you'd expect given his lack of game power. We had many internal conversations over what that meant—just like we had many conversations over how to project him in 2019—and basically left him his ranking intact in deference to the copious amount of live looks that pointed to a plus hit tool.

Variance: High. We're concerned about the hit tool collapsing at the highest levels, although he has obvious bench/utility fallbacks if things sour given his speed and versatility.

Mark Barry's Fantasy Take: Not sure if you've caught on by now, but it's hard to find steals in standard-roto formats. Edwards is very fast, and has hit for average in the minors, but there's a real threat that no semblance of power will ever come, which leaves him in danger of having a Billy Hamilton (or worse) fantasy future.

8 Cole Wilcox RHP — OFP: 60 — ETA: 2023
Born: 07/14/99 — Age: 21 — Bats: R — Throws: R — Height: 6'5" — Weight: 232
Origin: Round 3, 2020 Draft (#80 overall)

The Report: When Wilcox was included in the Snell trade, some analyses dismissed him as some distant ho-hum third-round pick. That is a gross mischaracterization, as his signing bonus would indicate, receiving essentially what would have been the 20th overall slot. The big righty out of Georgia had some of the best stuff in the draft. His issue(s) were mostly derived from an inefficient delivery that led to below-average control. When dialed-in, it's a heavy fastball that can reach 100 with a sharp slider and sinking power changeup. Early indicators from the spring showed a refined delivery with better control at the cost of a tick less velocity.

Development Track: Reports from Padres instructs prior to the trade had Wilcox up to 97 with many of the same qualities seen during his draft-eligible sophomore year. If you could point to the two organizations that are perhaps best equipped with getting pitchers to harness their elite power arsenal, it would be the Pads and Rays. In either case, he's in good hands and has a very high ceiling.

Variance: High. If it turns out he's more the player he was as a frosh, then he's more likely to be a freak in the 'pen. If the more recent version is closer to his true outcome, it's an easy call as a well above-average starter with star traits. --- Keanan Lamb

Mark Barry's Fantasy Take: Wilcox's profile screams "BULK GUY" in this organization. That's still useful, for sure, but it limits his fantasy upside.

9. Greg Jones SS   OFP: 55   ETA: 2022
Born: 03/07/98   Age: 23   Bats: S   Throws: R   Height: 6'2"   Weight: 175
Origin: Round 1, 2019 Draft (#22 overall)

The Report: Jones presents one of the more unique profiles you'll find of any top-200 prospect. Drafted as an ultra-fast college shortstop with projection, his physical measurements make you think he'd be this monster with five tool potential. In reality, while his switch-hitting ability might allow him to get on-base at an advanced clip, nothing other than his 70-plus grade speed is clearly above average. It's more line-drive power with plenty of extra-base hits mixed in, and his defense is okay enough to stay up the middle. If he hits anywhere near his first pro foray in short-season he could be a top-of-the-order threat.

Development Track: Jones could end up anywhere on the field. He played some center field at the Cape, some scouts think he's more suited at second base, but in the end it's inconsequential where he plays since he'll be fine. If the hit tool and on-base skills continue trending upward, his speed will allow him to play anywhere the Rays need to shoe-horn him in. Which, in a system as abundant as theirs, having a flexible player like this is incredibly valuable.

Variance: High. At his floor, he's a serviceable bench player with clear skills to be utilized. If the contact rates remain elevated given his speed he should be a good everyday player.

Mark Barry's Fantasy Take: I'd have Jones closer to Bruján in terms of dynasty. He might not have Edwards's wheels, but I think it's more likely that Jones will get on base at a decent clip and could even sock a dinger or two. Perhaps it's splitting hairs, but for me Jones is a top-75 or so fantasy prospect.

10 **Josh Lowe CF**   OFP: 55   ETA: Late 2021/Early 2022
Born: 02/02/98   Age: 23   Bats: L   Throws: R   Height: 6'4"   Weight: 205
Origin: Round 1, 2016 Draft (#13 overall)

The Report: Originally drafted as a prep third baseman, the Rays converted Lowe to center field the following season and he's taken to it quite well. His plus speed and arm work well on the grass, and despite only playing the outfield for a few seasons, he projects as an overall above-average defender there. Lowe's plus raw pop would have played fine as a corner infielder, but it makes the bat potentially special in center field. However, hit tool questions remain as Lowe has swing-and-miss issues with spin. But even if he only manages to Xerox his Double-A line further up the ladder, .250 and 20 bombs as an above-average center fielder is a good everyday guy.

Development Track: Lowe spent time at the alternate site and should be in the mix for reps in Tampa at some point in 2021. A Kevin Kiermaier trade might not exactly clear the path right away, but if he gets off to a good start in Triple-A and shows some improvement against higher-quality spin, it will be tough to justify keeping him off the carpet at the Trop.

Variance: Medium. Lowe has had some Double-A success already and the pop, speed, and glove all line up well for at least a fringe starter role, although the potential issues with southpaws and spin might limit the upside.

Mark Barry's Fantasy Take: There must have been a rule about having more than one member of the Lowe family in the lineup, as the Rays shipped out Nate so Josh could fly. Or whatever. Josh Lowe has power, speed, and the ability to work a walk. If he scales back on the swing-and-miss, he could be an impact fantasy option, taken in the first 3-4 rounds for years to come. If he doesn't, then maybe he's Drew Stubbs?

The Prospects You Meet Outside This Top Ten

Several more OFP 55s in somewhat particular order

Blake Hunt   C   Born: 11/10/98   Age: 22   Bats: R   Throws: R   Height: 6'3"   Weight: 215   Origin: Round 2, 2017 Draft (#69 overall)

The third prospect piece in the Snell deal, Hunt had a bit of a star turn in instructs, showcasing hard contact and advanced defensive skills. He always projected as a plus defensive catcher and showed plus raw pop, but his swing and plate discipline limited how much of it he could get into games. We need to see the new look bat in minor league games before calling this a full breakout, but Hunt looks like he might be the next prep catching prospect made good.

Brendan McKay   LHP   Born: 12/18/95   Age: 25   Bats: L   Throws: L   Height: 6'2"   Weight: 220   Origin: Round 1, 2017 Draft (#4 overall)

McKay is in a similar spot to A.J. Puk in the Oakland system: they both had labrum surgery during the season. Given the seriousness of labrum issues, that dropped both of them off the Top 101, but where that drop didn't even move Puk out of the top spot in the A's system, it drops McKay all the way out of the Top 10 here, which is a testament to the extreme system depth. If healthy, McKay's fastball/curveball combo and pitchability should make him a mid-rotation starter very quickly, but until he has a clean bill of health and is throwing well again we can't fully project that out yet.

Ronaldo Hernández   C   Born: 11/11/97   Age: 23   Bats: R   Throws: R   Height: 6'1"   Weight: 230   Origin: International Free Agent, 2014

A converted infielder, Hernández has above-average potential as a two-way catcher, but his defense needs to continue to improve, and he needs to tame his approach to get more of his plus raw pop into games against higher level pitching. The exposure to higher level pitching didn't functionally happen outside of the Rays alternate site in 2020, so we'll see where we are next year. He's dropped a little ordinally because of improvements around him in the system, but we think he's the same OFP 55 prospect.

Nick Bitsko   RHP   Born: 06/16/02   Age: 19   Bats: R   Throws: R   Height: 6'4"   Weight: 225   Origin: Round 1, 2020 Draft (#24 overall)

During the organizing process of putting together this extensive list for the Rays, Bitsko was easily within the top 5-7 prospects as one of the best prep pitchers in last year's draft. However, whenever you talk about injuries to pitchers you specifically want to avoid, it's anything involving the shoulder. After he had surgery to repair his labrum in December, he is questionable to pitch in 2021 after not pitching the spring of his draft year. That would be two full years off from competitive action. The big righty, when healthy, has mid-90's heat with projection for more, although at this juncture we hope for a full recovery to at least get back to where he was before.

Joe Ryan   RHP   Born: 06/05/96   Age: 25   Bats: R   Throws: R   Height: 6'2"   Weight: 205   Origin: Round 7, 2018 Draft (#210 overall)

After a downright dominant 2019 across three levels, Ryan made our 2020 Rays Top Ten and looked poised to … well, be 2020's Josh Fleming. I don't know the vagaries of the Rays baseball ops decisions, but you could argue Ryan's stuff isn't quite as good as that gaudy 38 percent K-rate. The fastball and curve are more above-average than true plus, and the cutter and change lag behind them. Ryan does throw all of them in the zone effectively, and there's certainly plenty of room for him on the 2021 Rays' pitching staff nowadays.

Drew Strotman   RHP   Born: 09/03/96   Age: 24   Bats: R   Throws: R   Height: 6'3"   Weight: 195   Origin: Round 4, 2017 Draft (#109 overall)

Strotman was our 2018 Low Minors Sleeper in this system. I saw him post-draft as a polished four-pitch righty, who touched 96 and had three average-to-above secondaries. He looked like he would fit well as a bulk-innings arm down the line. Well, the bulk part was a problem as he's thrown only 90 innings total since that 2017 season in the Penn League. Tommy John cost him most of 2018 and 2019, but he popped back up this year, healthy and sitting mid-90s. The slider and curve both look above-average, and yeah maybe the Rays still use him as a bulk innings guy given the durability concerns, but it's mid-rotation starter stuff.

Pedro Martinez   SS   Born: 01/28/01   Age: 20   Bats: S   Throws: R   Height: 5'11"   Weight: 165   Origin: International Free Agent, 2018

Acquired for 22 Jose Martinez plate appearances, Martinez was the seventh-best prospect in the Cubs' system coming into the season. We have no reason to think he's any worse and he doesn't crack the Rays' Top 15 or so. A speedy, hit-tool driven switch-hitting infielder who could probably play a few different spots competently, he's the platonic ideal of a Rays solid-average position player prospect. He hasn't seen full-season ball yet, but there's potential for more than just solid-average projection if he grows into some power and hits in A-ball.

Seth Johnson   RHP   Born: 09/19/98   Age: 22   Bats: R   Throws: R   Height: 6'1"   Weight: 200   Origin: Round 1, 2019 Draft (#40 overall)

Johnson is an infield convert with a plus-plus fastball, a plus-flashing slider, and significant questions about how he will hold up in the pros under a starter's workload. Obviously those weren't answered in 2020 and he's the highest variance prospect in this tier, non-shoulder-surgery division.

Heriberto Hernandez   C   Born: 12/16/99   Age: 21   Bats: R   Throws: R   Height: 6'1"   Weight: 180   Origin: International Free Agent, 2017

What if I told you the Rays traded for a player from the Rangers who 90 percent of people didn't know about, but the 10 percent who did cursed under their breath. Probably "Yeah idiot, I already knew about Pete Fairbanks." No, this is the sequel to that hit indie film. Hernandez is a Class-A outfielder with power to burn and development time needed to craft the rest into a functional MLB player. He'd be a great fit in an organization who understands talent maximization and patience for its ... well you get the idea. He's a Ray now, which means in three years he'll probably get a clutch hit in a playoff series while most of the country scratches their head and Googles. Not you, dear reader. You will know, and you will be prepared.

Brent Honeywell Jr.   RHP   Born: 03/31/95   Age: 26   Bats: R   Throws: R   Height: 6'2"   Weight: 195   Origin: Round 2, 2014 Draft (#72 overall)

Honeywell underwent his fourth elbow surgery in the last three years in December. Once a three-time Top 25 prospect, now he hasn't officially been on the rubber since the end of the 2017 season, although he's thrown some bullpens at times. In theory he had top-of-the-rotation stuff the last time he saw him and will be back on the mound in 2021, although he's going to be 26 by the time the season starts and we have no idea if his elbow can hold up.

Kevin Padlo   3B   Born: 07/15/96   Age: 24   Bats: R   Throws: R   Height: 6'2"   Weight: 210   Origin: Round 5, 2014 Draft (#143 overall)

A swing change at the end of 2019 to maximize his power certainly succeeded as Padlo slugged a career-high .538. But there are never solutions, always tradeoffs. Padlo can pop up a lot of pitches, and with most of the league going to high heaters this can be exploited. While he has above-average arm strength, he is slow footed at third and may be a better fit at first in an everyday role. This is another high-variance prospect in this organization. If it all clicks he is a middle-of-the-order thumper who splits between corner infield positions. If it doesn't, he may end up mashing in Korea.

Neraldo Catalina   RHP   Born: 06/21/00   Age: 21   Bats: R   Throws: R   Height: 6'6"   Weight: 202   Origin: International Free Agent, 2018

Catalina has plenty of upside and is starting to get to it. He is much more physical now, as he has started to fill out his lean, 6-foot-6 frame. The fastball velocity is among the best in the system, a mid-to-high 90s pitch with quality extension. The curveball velocity has ticked up as well and is now a power pitch with hard downer depth. Given this velocity and power of the breaker, it is difficult to locate at present, often spiked, but can also elicit some bad swings. Catalina needs innings, and could be pushed aggressively to Low-A to start '21.

And now a selection of OFP 50s

Josh Fleming   LHP   Born: 05/18/96   Age: 25   Bats: R   Throws: L   Height: 6'2"   Weight: 220   Origin: Round 5, 2017 Draft (#139 overall)

Speaking of Fleming, the crafty lefty was a bit of a surprise call up given the starting pitching depth in the system, but he pounded the zone with his bowling-ball, low-90s sinker, four or five innings at a time, and kept the ball on the ground and let the Rays' infield defense do it's work. He offers a pretty good sinking change as well to mitigate any platoon issues. I don't know if he can continue to suppress hits to this level, and both DRA and FIP thought the sub-3.00 ERA was unsustainable. But they also both thought he was at least an average arm. Score another one for Tampa's player dev.

Alika Williams   Born: 03/12/99   Age: 22   Bats: R   Throws: R   Height: 6'2"   Weight: 180   Origin: Round CBA, 2020 Draft (#37 overall)

If there is a "type" it seems the Rays have been targeting recently with college players, it's high contact/low strikeout players with track records. A three-year starter at Arizona State, surrounded by the likes of Hunter Bishop, Spencer Torkelson, among others, Williams served as a table-setter and steady defender for the Sun Devils. At present he's more of a glove-first option with confidence he'll stay at shortstop, although less confidence the offense will allow him to start everyday, even if buried at the back of the lineup.

Taylor Walls   SS   Born: 07/10/96   Age: 24   Bats: S   Throws: R   Height: 5'10"   Weight: 185   Origin: Round 3, 2017 Draft (#79 overall)
Walls has strong skills, but when looking at the final report he doesn't really stand out for a tool that is above-average. A switch-hitter with quality plate discipline, Walls is a tough out as he has above-average barrel control and works the whole field. A lot of the contact is of the low line drive style, so while he can hit the ball hard, there won't be a lot of home run power. The speed is average home to first, but it's enough to allow him to steal bases and cover ground well defensively. He has played second, short, and third in the minors, but will look to get some outfield work this upcoming season to add even more versatility—the Rays like this sort of thing.

Michael Plassmeyer   LHP   Born: 11/05/96   Age: 24   Bats: L   Throws: L   Height: 6'2"   Weight: 197   Origin: Round 4, 2018 Draft (#118 overall)
Putting Plassmeyer's measurables on this website doesn't make him stand out as much as if you see him in person. A low-slot lefty who throws strikes, this is a pitcher type that the Rays have had plenty of success with. He has a lot of deception in the delivery, which allows his otherwise mediocre fastball to be extremely effective. Similar to Ryan Yarbrough or Fleming, the changeup is his best offspeed pitch with late diving action that elicits its fair share of weak contact and swings and misses. As an advanced arm with a relatively high floor, Plassmeyer has a strong chance to make a debut this season.

Niko Hulsizer   OF   Born: 02/01/97   Age: 24   Bats: R   Throws: R   Height: 6'2"   Weight: 225   Origin: Round 18, 2018 Draft (#554 overall)
A big outfielder with big—read: plus-plus—raw, Hulsizer is a three-true-outcome bat whose swing-and-miss proclivities haven't been truly tested against upper minors pitching yet. The suite of defensive tools are average, so he's spent almost all his time in a corner outfield spot, and left is probably the best fit. So the walks and pop will have to keep showing up in the stat sheet to make him a regular in the bigs.

Top Talents 25 and Under (as of 4/1/2021):

1. Wander Franco, SS
2. Willy Adames, SS
3. Randy Arozarena, OF
4. Austin Meadows, OF
5. Shane Baz, RHP

6. Luis Patiño, RHP
7. Francisco Mejía, C
8. Vidal Bruján, IF
9. Shane McClanahan, LHP
10. Xavier Edwards, SS/2B

Yes, there's even more high-end young talent in the majors. Willy Adames would be ahead of nearly every prospect in baseball, but Franco is the best prospect in baseball. He was our No. 15 prospect himself in 2018, and is just a few points of batting average (or more national exposure) away from being a two-way star. And he's not even the best young shortstop in the system, somehow.

Austin Meadows had a bad 2020 after an All-Star 2019. He battled an oblique injury and missed some time with COVID-19, so we're assuming this is a blip and expecting him to run it back in 2021, where he blasted 33 home runs and a 135 DRC+. When healthy, he's an all-around offensive force.

Francisco Mejía needed a chance of scenery, and it came in the Snell trade. The 2018 No. 5 prospect is only 25, and he was actually fine in part-time duty in 2019. But the Padres just didn't seem to have any faith in him. It was only a few years ago that we saw him as baseball's next star catcher, and Tampa Bay is a very good place for him to try to turn it around.

Part 3: Featured Articles

Rays All-Time Top 10 Players

by Matthew Trueblood

POSITION PLAYERS

CARLOS PEÑA, 1B (2007-2010, 2012)
Thoughtful and personable, Peña drifted through three organizations where neither his off-the-field presence nor his on-field skills were properly appreciated despite his status as a former first-round draft pick (10th overall in 1998). When he landed with Joe Maddon's Rays, everything clicked. He matured into an elite power hitter, with a beautiful, long left-handed stroke and exacting plate discipline. Though he played just four years with Tampa during his first stint, he managed 144 homers (leading the AL in 2009) and drew 373 walks. In the field, his actions were smooth, and he had unusual range. His 2007, which included .292/.411/.627 rates, 46 home runs, and 103 walks, was superb though well out of line with the rest of his career. A return in 2012 after a year away proved to be one too many trips to the well.

AUBREY HUFF, 3B/1B/OF, 2000-2006
A lefty at the plate, Huff bloomed late, but had a strong run for miserable early Devil Rays teams. From 2002-04, he was a good hitter but lacked a defensive home. Tampa tried him in left field, third base, first base, and as the designated hitter, but only found him up to the snuff defensively at the last of those. Still, he hit .307/.364/.524 over that three-year peak, before inconsistency seized him and the Devil Rays quickly shipped him out of town.

EVAN LONGORIA, 3B, 2008-2017
When it comes to the modern hitting paradigm, Longoria was a bit ahead of the curve. His swing and approach were geared to generate fly balls, but especially, to pull them to left field. He did it extremely well for almost a decade in Tampa Bay, serving not only as the greatest Ray ever, but also as the symbol of their

rapid transition from laughingstock to perennial contender. A 126 DRC+ as a rookie in 2008 would be his lowest until 2014—he still won the AL Rookie of the Year aw and he was a highly athletic, strong-armed Gold Glover of a third baseman.

JULIO LUGO, SS, 2003-2006
Everything about Lugo's association with the Rays was unfortunate, coming about because it took place during a less-aware era than ours though it wasn't very long ago in real terms. A product of the Astros system who reached the majors in 2000, he was released in May 2003 after being arrested following a horrifying attack on his wife. Then-commissioner Bud Selig washed his hands and the Rays had no compunctions about picking up the pieces. What they got was almost irrelevant: Lugo delivered three solid seasons of balanced play. He was a lithe, quick shortstop, had slightly above-average power for the position, and made plenty of contact. He also stole 88 bases in 113 tries. None of that stopped the 2003-06 Devil Rays from losing a total of 386 games, but he made them more watchable, if harder to stomach.

CARL CRAWFORD, OF, 2002-2010
Crawford was the first homegrown star for the Devil Rays and stuck around long enough to be one of the engines of the Rays' success. Hitting from a wide-open, spread-out crouch, he swung hard every time, looking to clear his hip and yank the ball to right field. His terrific speed was always visible; he was not the kind of effortless athlete whose talent camouflages itself. An early darling of new-age defensive metrics, he won three of the first four Fielding Bible Awards for left field. His quick decline after leaving the Rays prevented him from piling up counting stats, but that in no way invalidates his earlier stardom.

MELVIN UPTON, JR OF/SS (2004-2012)
A former number-one overall pick, Upton had very high expectations to meet, and couldn't always finagle it. He wasn't an infielder no matter how desperately the Rays wanted him to be one. Strikeouts plagued him, though when the rest of his game was working they didn't derail him. In his six full seasons in Tampa, he had an above-average DRC+ five times, stole at least 31 bases five times (and 22 in the worst year for those), thrice topped 23 homers, drew more than his share of walks, and led the league in frustration—as long as one counts both frustration inflicted on opponents and that visited upon one's own team.

MATT JOYCE, OF (2009-2014)
The idea that a team would do best not to even pick up the phone when the Rays call began to percolate sometime around the point when the Tigers traded Joyce to Tampa Bay for Edwin Jackson. It was a perfectly fair deal. Jackson was fine for the Tigers and had four years of team control remaining, but the team traded

him after just one of those. Meanwhile, Joyce became a staple in Joe Maddon's Stengelian platoon system on the outfield corners. Though never a full-timer, and never more than an average defensive right fielder, Joyce piled up value from 2010 through 2014, hitting .251/.344/.434 even as offense plunged league-wide.

DESMOND JENNINGS, OF (2010-2016)

For a little while it seemed as though the Rays' wells of homegrown talent would never be exhausted; they could simply install a new star-caliber young guy every time one departed via trade or free agency. Jennings marked the end of that era, not because he wasn't another top prospect, but because this time, the prospect did what so many of them do: come up, perform at an average level for a couple of years, then fizzle and fade quickly. He managed a defense-driven 6.0 total WARP from 2012-14, but the tools and skills never quite came together.

KEVIN KIERMAIER, OF (2013-PRESENT)

Kiermaier hasn't qualified for the batting title since 2015. He's only posted a DRC+ of average or better once, and it was 101, in 2017. Yet he comfortably makes this list more because of his own skills than because of Tampa Bay's short and checkered team history. At his best, Kiermaier was a world-beating defensive center fielder. He won his second Fielding Bible Award there in 2020, and center field is a position where the battle for that honor is perennially fierce. As he demonstrated during Tampa's deep 2020 playoff run, he's also capable of coming up with huge hits at times, even if his overall offensive output is tepid.

BEN ZOBRIST, EVERYWHERE (2006-2014)

The notion that Joe Maddon created (or even innovated) a new role for Zobrist is silly. There have been star-caliber multi-position players throughout baseball history; we have merely learned to notice and celebrate them better. Still, Zobrist did seem to bring that archetype back from expansion- and PED-enforced obscurity, and all the pieces of his game fit nicely into the gig. He was a fidgety, hunching switch-hitter with a distinctly plainspoken demeanor, but those things tended to hide his impressive size, long-striding speed, and solid power. He was an OBP machine, a great defender at four or five positions, and a heady baserunner. By deploying him as he did, Maddon made the most of all of that.

PITCHERS

ROLANDO ARROJO, RHP (1998-1999)

Conceptually, the Cuban Arrojo was the fledgling Devil Rays' answer to El Duque or a version of José Contreras before the U.S. got José Contreras. In practice, he had a fine ride on Tampa Bay's maiden voyage, a much bumpier one in 1999, and then was shipped off to Colorado so the Devil Rays could acquire the aging

Vinny Castilla. In the meantime, though, he was the first Tampa Bay pitcher to get a win and used his four-pitch mix to limit the damage associated with being an expansion team in the AL East.

SCOTT KAZMIR, LHP (2004-2008)

The deal that sent mediocre starter Victor Zambrano to the Mets in July 2004, at the cost of Kazmir (who had been New York's top draft pick just two years earlier), is still a sore spot in Queens. Quite unlike the sinker-slinging veteran version who would pop back up later, the young Kazmir was a strikeout monster whose slider and changeup were each potential out pitches and who could spin a four-seamer up like few of his contemporaries. He won a strikeout title in 2007 and became one of the symbols of Tampa Bay's savviness when they emerged as contenders the following year.

JAMES SHIELDS, RHP (2006-2012)

Famously competitive and intense, Shields became the heart of the Rays' pivot from struggling expansion team to perennial contenders. He bought into Maddon's way of running the team (and into the front office's vision) enough to sign an early, team-friendly extension, and then he helped make them the kind of team for which he wanted to pitch. He owned a true five-pitch mix and could command them all well enough to keep hitters defensive. He pitched to the shifted defenses behind him, worked deep into games, and helped teammates develop the same habits and skills that made him great.

DAVID PRICE, LHP (2008-2014)

Price was the first in a string of top overall draft picks who were considered no-brainers and he has more than met that high standard. It's remarkable how quickly he found success, because at the beginning of his career he mostly threw his crackling fastball and a couple of middling, amorphous breaking balls. As he matured, though, he switched from the four-seamer to a power sinker as his primary fastball, added the cutter, which became his out pitch, and developed the devastating changeup that turned him into a Cy Young winner. He's huge and physically gifted, but he's lived up to his billing because of great, intelligent craftsmanship.

MATT GARZA, RHP (2009-2010)

Emotions were never far below the surface for Garza. He occasionally lost control of them, but more often, he pitched with them, made them part of his game, and could be a joy to watch because of them. Like the pitcher (Chris Archer) for whom he would be traded, he featured a power breaking ball with sharp downward action. Unlike Chris Archer (below), he had feel for three or four pitches when going well, and generally matched his topline results to his peripherals. He only pitched three seasons in Tampa, but thanks especially to his dominant 2008 ALCS showing, and to the trades that brought him and moved him on (the latter of which brought Archer), he felt like a bigger part of their history.

JEREMY HELLICKSON, RHP (2010-2014)

Throwing a steady diet of changeups kept hitters off of Hellickson's average stuff longer than one might have expected. They still figured him out, but by the time they did so, he'd posted a 3.06 ERA in his first 400 big-league innings and won the 2011 American League Rookie of the Year Award. The velocity gaps between his fastball, changeup, and curve were all so large that, once hitters drew a bead on him, they could tee off, but those patterns take time to pin down.

ALEX COBB, RHP (2011-2017)

Postwar righty fireman Harry "Fritz" Dorish used to throw a slip pitch with the fading action of a screwball, which some called "The Thing." Any time a pitch earns that moniker, it's good news, and that's what many called Cobb's split-change (ahem) thing when he was at his best. Count it, perhaps, as troubling reinforcement of the evidence that certain styles of splitter lead to arm trouble, because Cobb had much of that, but when he was on the mound and had his full repertoire, he was nasty.

CHRIS ARCHER, RHP (2012-2018)

Archer made himself an electrifying pitching prospect; the Rays helped make him a full-fledged star pitcher. With a nasty fastball-slider combination, but little else, and without superb control, Archer came to Tampa Bay as the headliner (but by no means the only credible piece) in the deal that sent Matt Garza to the Cubs. Without adding a third pitch, though, Archer turned into a dominant starter within two years, because the Rays kept encouraging him to throw that biting, vertical slider increasingly often. From 2015-17, he fanned an average of 245 batters per year, and added 14.9 WARP.

JAKE ODORIZZI, RHP (2013-2017)

With good rise on his heat and a splitter that mirrored its spin nicely, Odorizzi could not merely miss bats but make hitters look foolish. His control was far better than his command, though, which often meant too many hittable pitches wandering over the plate. It wasn't until after he left Tampa Bay that he found the wiggle he needed to better manage contact and consistently rack up strikeouts. Twice through a batting order, though, he did yeoman's work, and the Rays' decision to trade him was one of the uglier instances of penny-pinching in team history.

BLAKE SNELL, LHP (2016-2020)

It took a little over a year for Snell to put together the many thrilling pieces of his repertoire in the optimal way, and after the glorious, Cy Young-winning season in which he did so, elbow trouble crept in. Still, by the end of 2020, it was back on full display: a high-spin fastball, multiple forms of vertical and lateral movement, and improving command, tied together by an athletic delivery and unwavering self-confidence. Lifting him from Game 6 of the World Series will be in Kevin Cash's obituary, which seems cruel, but it's fitting: that move spelled the end of Snell's time in Tampa Bay, even though it didn't cost the Rays a ring.

A Taxonomy of 2020 Abnormalities

by Rob Mains

I'm going to start this with a trivia question. Trust me, it's relevant. Don't bother skipping to the end of the article to find the answer, it's not there.

Only five players have appeared in 140 or more games for 16 straight seasons. Who are they?

It's a trivia question starting off an essay, so you know how this works: Whatever you guessed, you're wrong. It's okay. As someone who purchased this book, chances are good that you're an educated baseball fan. But the circumstances behind 2020 force us to abandon, or at least seriously question, some of our favorite patterns and crutches for evaluating the game we love.

We just completed what was undoubtedly the strangest season in MLB history. No fans, geographically limited schedule, universal DH, seven-inning twin bills, runners on second in extra innings, a 16-team postseason, a club playing at a Triple-A stadium. Some of these changes will likely persist (sorry), but we've never had so many tweaks dumped on us all at once, at least not since they figured out how many balls were in a walk.

And the biggest, of course, was the 60-game season. The 19th century was dotted with teams that went bankrupt before the season ended, but the lone season with only 60 scheduled games was 1877. That year there were only six teams, the league rostered a total of 77 players (just 16 more than the 2020 Marlins), and batters called for pitches to be thrown high or low by the pitcher, who was 50 feet away. We can say the 2020 season was easily the shortest ever for recognizable baseball.

As such, it'll stand out. Few abbreviated seasons do. Just about everybody reading this knows the 1994 season ended after Seattle's Randy Johnson struck out Oakland's Ernie Young for the last out of the Mariners-A's game on August 11. The ensuing player strike wiped out the rest of the season and the postseason. Teams played only 112-117 games that year.

And many of you know that a strike in the middle of the 1981 season split the season in two, resulting in the only Division Series until 1995. Teams played only 103-111 games that year, the shortest regular season since 1885.

Those two seasons are memorable. So when we see that nobody drove in 100 runs in 1981, or that Greg Maddux was the only pitcher with 180 or more innings pitched in 1994, we think, "Of course. Strike year."

But we don't remember other short years. You might not recall that the 1994 strike spilled into the next year, chopping 18 games off the 1995 schedule. You might've read that the 1918 season, played during the last pandemic, ended after Labor Day due to the government's World War I "work or fight" order. A strike erased the first week and a half of the 1972 season, but that year's best known as the last time pitchers batted in the American League.

The point is, while we don't remember small changes to the schedule, we remember the big ones. The 1981 mid-season strike. The 1994 season- and Series-ending strike. And, of course, the pandemic-shortened 2020 season. We won't need a reminder why Marcell Ozuna's 18 homers were the fewest to lead the National League in a century. (Literally; Cy Williams led with 15 in 1920.)

Now, about that trivia question. The five players are Hank Aaron, Brooks Robinson, Pete Rose, Ichiro Suzuki, and Johnny Damon. The one nobody gets, of course, is Damon, and a lot of people miss Ichiro, whose last season of 140-plus games came garbed in the red-orange and ocean blue of Miami when he was 42. That's half of what makes it a good question. The other half is the two guys whom many think made the list but didn't. Lou Gehrig? His streak started in the Yankees' 42nd game of the 1925 season and lasted only 13 seasons after that. And everybody assumes Cal Ripken Jr. did it, having played 2,632 straight games over 17 seasons. But one of those 17 seasons was 1994, when the Orioles played only 112 games.

My point? *I just told you* everybody remembers the 1994 strike year, but everybody forgets it fell in the middle of Ripken's streak, separating the first twelve years from the last four. Just because we recall something doesn't mean it's always at the front of our minds.

Nobody is going to forget 2020, and baseball is obviously not the main reason. But there will come a time in the future when you're looking at a player's or a team's record, and there will be baffling numbers there for 2020, and you'll think, "I wonder what happened." (Not to mention the missing line for minor league players.) Just like you forgot that the 1994 strike limited Ripken to 112 games.

Try not to forget it, though. The 2020 season resulted in weird statistical results for several reasons.

There were only 60 games.
I know, duh. But that had impacts beyond counting stats like Ozuna's home run total or Yu Darvish and Shane Bieber leading the majors with eight wins. (I know, pitcher wins, but still.)

The 162-game season is the longest among major North American sports, and that duration gives us a gift. Over the course of a long season, small variations tend to even out. A player who has a ten-game hot streak will probably have a ten-game cold streak. A team that starts the year losing a bunch of close games will probably win a bunch of them. We get regression to the mean. Statistics stabilize.

Consider flipping a coin. Over the long run, we expect it to come up heads about half the time. But the fewer flips, the more variation there'll be. If you flip a coin six times, probability theory tells us you'll get at least two-third heads about 34 percent of the time. Flip it 30 times, your chance of two-thirds heads drops to five percent.

Or, relevant to this case, if you flip a coin 60 times, your chance of getting at least 36 heads—that's 60 percent—is 7.75 percent. Expand the coin-flipping to 162 times, and the chance of getting 60 percent heads drops to 0.73 percent.

In other words, the odds of an outcome that's 20 percent better (or worse) than expected is *more than ten times higher* when you flip your coin 60 times than when you do it 162 times. Call it small sample size, call lack of mean reversion, or call it luck not evening out, 162 is a lot more predictive than 60. You get much more variation over 60 games than over 162. Bieber's 1.63 ERA and 0.87 FIP aren't something we'd see over a full season, and neither is Javier Baéz's .203/.238/.360.

Some players' lines in 2020 look normal. Brian Anderson had an .811 OPS in 2019 and an .810 OPS in 2020. (He probably would have gotten that last point if he'd been given enough time.) But there are many like Bieber and Baéz, some of them from young players still establishing their talent levels. The answer to the question, "What went right or wrong for that guy in 2020?" is most likely "Nothing, it was just a 2020 thing."

Preseason training was abbreviated for hitters.

Every year, spring training drags. Players get tired of it, fans get tired of it, and you sure can tell sportswriters get tired of it. Yes, something to get everyone into shape is necessary, but does it really have to drag on for over a month? Can't we shorten it?

The 2020 season answered in the negative, at least for hitters. Warren Spahn is credited with saying that hitting is timing and pitching is upsetting timing. It appears nobody had his timing down after the abbreviated July summer camp. Through August 9—18 games into the season—MLB batters were hitting .230/.311/.395 with a .275 BABIP. That BABIP, had it held, would have been the lowest since 1968, the Year of the Pitcher. In recent years it's hovered around .300.

It didn't hold. Play returned to more normal levels the rest of the year: .249/.325/.425 with a .297 BABIP starting August 10. But batters whose play concentrated in those first two weeks wound up with ugly lines. Andrew

Benintendi went on the injured list with a season-ending rib cage strain on August 11. His final line: .103/.314/.128 in 14 games. Franchy Cordero went on the IL with a hamate bone fracture on August 9 and a .154/.185/.231 line. Even though he came back strong in a late September return, it was too late to repair his full-season numbers.

Preseason training was abbreviated for pitchers.

Every year, spring training drags. Players get tired of it, fans get tired of it ... wait, I already said that. But the abbreviated preseason was tough on pitchers, too. As noted, they had the upper hand coming out of the gate. But then they lost that hand. And then their arms, too.

The 2020 season was spread over 67 days. During those 67 days, 237 pitchers hit the Injured List, compared to 135 in the first 67 days of 2019. A lot of those IL stints, though, were COVID-19-related. Still, over the first 67 days of the 2019 season, there were 72 pitchers on the IL with arm injuries. That figure jumped to 110 in 2020, a 53 percent increase.

There are a number of factors contributing to pitcher arm injuries, ranging from usage to velocity, but it appears that attenuated preseason training played a role. A lot of pitchers had super-short seasons due to arm woes. Corey Kluber, Roberto Osuna, and Shohei Ohtani combined for seven innings, none after August 8. All suffered arm injuries. We'll never know whether they'd have fared better with a longer preseason, but we can guess how they probably feel.

Everybody played.

Rosters were set to expand from 25 to 26 in 2020, so even if we'd had a normal season, we'd have likely seen 2019's record of 1,410 players on MLB rosters broken. But due to the pandemic, rosters started the year at 30 and were cut to only 28. Add multiple COVID-19 absences and the revolving door caused by poor starts by hitters and a rash of pitcher arm injuries, and 1,289 players appeared in MLB games in 2020. The comparable figure over the first 67 days of the 2019 season was 1,109. That 16 percent increase works out to an average of six more players per team in 2020 compared to a similar slice of 2019. A future look back at 2020 rosters will include a lot of unfamiliar names.

Plus became a minus.

In advanced metrics, we adjust batter and pitcher performance for park and league/era variations. A plus sign appended to the end of a measure means that it's adjusted for park and league. It's scaled to an average of 100, with higher figures above average and lower figures below average. (Similarly, a metric with a minus is also park- and league-adjusted and scaled to 100, with lower values better.) Here at BP, our advanced measure of offensive performance is DRC+. Baseball-Reference has OPS+ and FanGraphs has wRC+.

Using park and league adjustments, we can compare Dante Bichette's 1995 Steroid Era season at pre-humidor Coors Field (.340/.364/.620, 40 homers, 128 RBI, MVP runner-up) with Jim Wynn's 1968 Year of the Pitcher season at the cavernous Astrodome (.269/.376/.474, 26 homers, 67 RBI, no MVP votes). It's not close. DRC+, OPS+, and wRC+ all give the nod to Wynn, handily. This is a useful tool. As my Baseball Prospectus colleague Patrick Dubuque tweeted last fall, "Please note that when I ask how you are, I am already adjusting for era."

The 2020 season messes up plus (and minus) stats for two reasons. First, the park adjustment was based on only 30 home games instead of the usual 81. Everything noted above regarding the short season applies, literally doubly, to park effect calculations. DRC+ uses a single-season park factor. OPS+ uses a three-year average and wRC+ five years. The figure for 2020 is suspect.

Second, OPS+ and wRC+ adjust for league: American and National. (DRC+ adjusts for opponent, regardless of league.) While there were two leagues in 2020, they were an artificial construct. To reduce travel, teams played opponents geographically, not based on league. There weren't two leagues, American and National. There were three, Western, Central, and Eastern.

That makes a difference because teams in the same league played in different run-scoring environments. AL teams scored 4.58 runs per game, NL teams 4.71. That's a small difference. But teams in the East scored 0.21 more runs per game (4.95) than teams in the West (4.74), and they both scored a lot more than Central teams (4.25). Adjusting for league misses that difference, so this book will be safe in that regard, but other sources may be distorted somewhat.

Not every game was a "game."
In 2020, the rising tide of strikeouts was finally stemmed. Strikeouts per team per game fell from 8.8 in 2019 to 8.7 in 2020. That marked the first decline after 14 straight annual increases.

In 2020, the rising tide of strikeouts rose higher. Batters struck out in 23.4 percent of plate appearances compared to 23.0 percent in 2019. That marked the 15th straight annual increase.

Both are true statements.

Because of two rule changes—seven-inning doubleheaders and runners on second in extra innings—games in 2020 were unprecedented in their brevity. There were 37.0 plate appearances per game in 2020. The only years with fewer were 1904 and 1906-1909. The average game in 2020 entailed 8.61 innings pitched, the fewest since 1899.

So when you see any per-game stats for 2020, you need to increase them by 3 or 4 percent to get them on equal footing with recent years.

Tampa Bay Rays 2021

Or, better, just ignore them. Last year happened. There were major league games contested between major league teams. But when you're looking at those physical or electronic baseball cards, when you're weaving narratives over why this young player's inevitable rise to stardom fell apart or why that old veteran rekindled his magic, don't linger on the 2020 line. It was just too weird.

Thanks to Lucas Apostoleris for research assistance.

—Rob Mains is an author of Baseball Prospectus.

Tranches of WAR

by Russell A. Carleton

We ask "replacement level" to be a lot of things. Sometimes contradictory things. Sometimes I wonder if we know what it even means anymore. The original idea was that it represented the level of production that a team could expect to get from "freely available talent", including bench players, minor leaguers, and waiver wire pickups. It created a common benchmark to compare everyone to, and for that reason, it represented an advancement well beyond what was available at the time. In fact, it created a language and a framework for evaluating players that was not just better but *entirely* different than what came before it.

But then we started mumbling in that language. The idea behind "wins above replacement" was one part sci-fi episode and one part mathematical exercise. Imagine that a player had disappeared before the season and suddenly, in an alternate timeline, his team would have had to replace him. The distance between him and that replacement line was his value. We need to talk about that alternate timeline.

Without getting too into 2:00 am "deep conversations" with extensive navel-gazing, it's worth thinking about why one player might not be playing, while another might.

- A player might not be playing because he has a short-term injury or his manager believes that he needs a day off.
- A player might not be playing because he has a longer-term injury that requires him to be on the injured list.

There's a difference here between these two situations. In particular, the first one generally *doesn't* involve a compensatory roster move, while the second one does. It's possible, though not guaranteed, that the person who will be replacing the injured/resting player would be the same in either case. That matters. Teams generally carry a spare part for all eight position players on the diamond, although in the era of a four-player bench, those spare parts usually are the backup plan for more than one spot.

A couple of years ago, I posed a hypothetical question. Suppose that a team had two players in its system fighting for a fourth outfielder spot. One of them was a league average hitter, but would be worth 20 runs below average if allowed to play center field for a full season. One of them was a perfectly average fielder, but would be 15 runs below average as a hitter, if allowed to play an entire season. Which of the two should the team roster? It's tempting to say the second one, as overall, he is the better player. That misses the point. A league average hitter on the bench isn't just a potential replacement for an injured outfielder. He might also pinch hit for the light-hitting shortstop in a key spot. You keep the average hitter on the roster, even though he isn't a hand-in-glove fit for one specific place on the field, because being a bench player is a different job description than being a long-term fill-in for someone. If you find yourself in need of a longer-term fill-in, you can bring the other guy up from AAA.

When we're determining the value of an everyday player though, if he had disappeared before the season and a team would have had to replace his production, they likely would have done it with a player who was a long-term fill-in type because they would have had to replace a guy who played everyday. Maybe that's the same guy that they would have rostered on their bench anyway, but we don't know. It gets to the query of what we hope to accomplish with WAR. Are we looking for an accurate modeling of reality or are we looking for a common baseline to compare everyone to? Both have their uses, but they are somewhat different questions.

Let's talk about another dichotomy.

- A player might not be playing because he isn't very good and is a bench-level player.
- A player might not be playing because there is another player on the team who has a situational advantage that makes him the better choice today. The classic case of this is a handedness platoon. On another day, he might be a better choice.

When we think about player usage, I think we're still stuck in the model that there are starters and there are scrubs. We have plenty of words for bench players or reserves or backups or utility guys. We do still have the word "platoon" in our collective vocabulary, but in the age of short benches, it's hard to construct one. It's always been hard to construct them. You have to find two players who hit with different hands, have skill sets that complement each other, and probably play the same position. In the era of the short bench, one of them had probably better double as a utility player in some way. Baseball has a two-tiered language geared toward the idea of regulars and reserves. The fact that it was so easy for me to find plenty of synonyms for "a player whose primary function is to come into a game to replace a regular player if he is injured or resting" should tell you something.

I'm always one to look for "unspoken words" in baseball. What is it called when someone is both half of a platoon and the utility infielder? That guy exists sometimes, but he reveals himself in that role—usually by accident. We don't have a word for that, and whenever I find myself saying "we don't have a word for that", I look for new opportunities. What do you call it, further, when the job of being the utility infielder is decentralized across the whole infield with occasional contributions from the left fielder? It's not even a "super-utility" player. What happens when you build your entire roster around the idea that everyone will be expected to be a triple major?

⚾ ⚾ ⚾

I think someone else beat me to this one, and on a grand scale. Platoons work because we know that hitters of the opposite hand to the pitcher get better results than hitters of the same hand, usually to the tune of about 20 points of OBP. If you want to express that in runs, it usually comes out to somewhere around 10 to 12 runs of linear weights value prorated across 650 PA. But hang on a second, now let's say that we have two players who might start today, both of roughly equal merit with the bat. One has a handedness advantage, but is the worse fielder of the two. In that case, as long as his "over the course of a season" projection as a fielder at whatever position you want to slot him into is less than a 10-run drop from the guy he might replace, then he's a better option today.

We're not used to thinking of utility players as bat-first options, who would play below-average defense at three different infield positions. That guy might hook on as a 2B/3B/LF type (Howie Kendrick, come on down!) but teams usually think to themselves that they need as their utility infielder someone who "can handle" shortstop, the toughest of the infield spots to play. If someone can do that *and* hit well, he's probably already starting somewhere, so he's not available as a utility infielder. It's easier for those glove guys to find a job. In a world where the replacement for a shortstop *has to be* the designated utility infielder, that makes sense.

But as we talked about last week, we're living in a different world. The rate at which a replacement for a regular starter turns out to be *another starter* shifting over to cover has gone way up over the last five years. There was always some of it in the game, but this has been a supernova of switcheroos. Now if your second baseman is capable of playing a decent shortstop, that 2B/3B/LF guy can swap in. He's not actually playing shortstop, and maybe the defense suffers from the switch, but if he's got enough of a bat, he might outhit those extra fielding miscues. And in doing so, he is effectively your backup shortstop.

Somewhere along the lines, teams got hip to the idea of multi-positional play from their regulars. I've written before about how you can't just put a player, however athletic, into a new position and expect much at first. The data tell us that. Eventually, players can learn to be multi-positionalists, but it takes time, roughly on the order of two months, before they're OK. But there's a hidden message in there. If you give a player some reps at a new spot, he's a reasonably gifted athlete and somewhat smart and willing to learn, he could probably pick it up enough to get to "good enough," and it doesn't take forever. You just have to be purposeful about it. Maybe you get to the point where you can start to say "he's still below average but we could move him there and get another bat into the lineup, and it's a net win."

Teams have started to build those extra lessons into their player development program. It used to be seen as a mark of weakness to be relegated to "utility player" because that meant that you were a bench player (all those synonyms above come with a side of stigma). Now, it's a way of building a team. If you get a few reps in the minors (where it doesn't count) at a spot, you'll have at least played the spot at game speed before. There are limits to how far you can push that. A slow-footed "he's out in left field because we don't have the DH" guy is never going to play short, but maybe your third baseman can try second base and not look like a total moose out there.

⚾ ⚾ ⚾

Back to WAR. I'd argue that the world of starters and scrubs is slowly disintegrating, for good cause. In the event that a regular starter really does go down with an injury–ostensibly, the alternate universe scenario that WAR is attempting to model–it makes the team a little more resilient to replacing him. And the good news is that you're more likely to be able to replace him with the best of the bench bunch, rather than the third-best guy, because the best guy doesn't have to be an exact positional match for the guy who got hurt. And that's what the manager would want to do. He'd want to replace that long-term production, not with an amalgam of everyone else who played that position, but with the best guy available from his reserves.

Now this is still WAR. We still want to retain the principle that we should be measuring a player, and not his teammates. We need some sort of common baseline, and despite what I just said, we'll still need some sort of amalgam. To construct that, I give to you the idea of the tranche. The word, if you've not heard it before, refers to a piece of a whole that is somehow segmented off. It's often used in finance to talk about layers of a financial instrument.

Here, I want you to consider that there are 30 starters at each of the seven non-battery positions (catchers should have their own WAR, since only a catcher can replace a catcher). We can identify them by playing time, and we can futz around with the definition a little bit if we need to. Next, among those who aren't in that starting pool, we identify the top tranche of the 30 best bench players, which I would again identify by playing time, and then the second and third and fourth and so on. If a player were to disappear, his manager would probably want to take a guy from that top tranche of the bench to replace him. In a world where even the starters can slide around the field, that becomes more feasible.

We can take a look at that top tranche and say "How many of them showed that they are able to play (first, second, etc.)?" and therefore could have directly substituted for the starter? How many of them could have been a direct substitute for our injured player? We don't know whether one of them would be on *a specific* team, but we can say that 40 percent of the time, a manager would have been able to draw from tranche 1 in filling the role, and 35 percent from tranche 2. But on tranche 1, we can also look at how many of those players played a position that could have then shifted and covered for that spot. We'd need some eligibility criteria for all of this (probably a minimum number of games played) but it would just be a matter of multiplication. Shortstop would be harder to fill, and managers would probably be dipping a little further down in the talent pool, and so replacement level would be lower, as it is now.

Doing some quick analysis, I found that the difference in just batting linear weights (haven't even gotten into running or fielding) between tranche 1 and tranche 2 in 2019 was about 6.5 runs, prorated across 650 PA. Between tranche 1 and tranche 3, it's 10.8 runs. The ability to shift those plate appearances up the ladder has some real value.

This part is important. We can also give credit to starters for the positions that they showed an ability to play, even if they didn't play them (this is the guy fully capable of playing center, but who's in a corner because the team already has a good center fielder) because he allows a team to carry a player who hits like a left fielder to functionally be the team's backup center fielder. He facilitates that movement upward among the tranches. We can start to appreciate the difference between a left fielder who would never be able to hack it in center (and the compensatory move that his team would have to make) and the left fielder who could do it, but just didn't have to very often.

Past that, you can continue to use whatever hitting and fielding and running metrics you like to determine a player's value, but when we get down to constructing that baseline, I'd argue we need a better conceptual and mathematical framework. It's going to require some more #GoryMath than we're used to, but I'd argue it's a better conceptualization of the way that MLB actually plays the game in 2020. If…y'know…MLB plays in 2020. If WAR is going to be our flagship statistic among the *acronymati*, then we need to acknowledge that it contains some old and starting-to-be-out-of-date assumptions about the game. We may need to tinker with it. Here's my idea for how.

—*Russell A. Carleton is an author of Baseball Prospectus.*

Secondhand Sport

by Patrick Dubuque

Back before time stopped, I liked to go to thrift stores. Now that I'm older, I rarely ever buy anything—I don't need much in my life, now—but I still enjoy the old familiar circuit: check to see if there are baseball cards to write about, look for board or card games to play with the kids, scan for random ironic jerseys, hit the book section. It takes ten, maybe fifteen minutes. Thrift stores are the antithesis of modern online shopping, because you don't know what they have, and you don't even really know what you want. It's junk, literal junk, stuff other people thought was worthless. That's what makes it great.

In an idealized economy, thrift stores shouldn't exist. Everybody has a living wage, and every product has a durability that exactly matches its desired life; nothing should need to be given away, no one should need to be given to. But then, thrift stores shouldn't work on a customer experience level, either. You wouldn't think an ethos of "let's make everything disorganized and hard to find" would lead to customer satisfaction, but low-budget retailers like TJ Maxx and Ross thrive on this model. People like bargain hunting as much for the hunting as the bargain; it's part of the experience, spending time as if it's a wager. There's a thrill, occasionally, in inefficiency.

In sports, the modern overuse of the word "inefficiency" is a condemnation: It insinuates that there is *an* efficiency, a correct way to be found, and that all other ways are wrong ways. It's prevalent in baseball but hardly contained to it; the lifehack, the Silicon Valley disruption are other examples of productivity creep in our daily lives. Their modern success makes plenty of sense. Maximization of resources, after all, is its own puzzle, and an industry of European board games is founded upon it. It's fun to take a system and optimize it, unravel it like a sudoku puzzle. If there's only one kind of genius, after all, there's no way anyone can fail to appreciate it.

Baseball has been hacking away at these perceived inefficiencies since its inception: platoons, bullpens, farm systems were all installed to extract more out of the tools at hand. But it's been a particular badge of the sabermetric movement, from Ken Phelps and his All-Star Team to Ricardo Rincon and the darlings of *Moneyball*. It's business, but it's also an ethos: the idea that there's treasure among the trash, something we all failed to appreciate until someone brought it to light.

It's the myth that made Sidd Finch so enticing, that fuels so many "best shape" narratives and new pitch promises. We all, athletes and unathletic sportswriters, want to believe that there's genius trapped inside us, and that it's just a matter of puzzling out the combination to unlock it. That our art, our style is the next inefficiency, waiting for our own Billy Beane. It's why we root for underdogs, and why we're excited for the Mike Tauchmans and the Eurubiel Durazos, champions of skin-deep mediocrity.

Except we aren't anymore, really. The days of "Free X" have descended beyond the ring of irony and into obscurity. There are still Xs to be freed, or at least one X, duplicated endlessly: Mike Ford, Luke Voit, Max Muncy. The undervalued one-dimensional slugger demonstrated how the game hasn't quite culturally caught up to its logical extreme. But for those who don't fit the rather spacious mold, times are grimmer. As Rob Arthur revealed several months ago, there's been a marked increase in the number of sub-replacement relievers. It's the outcome of a greater number of teams forced to play out games without the talent to win them, but it's also emblematic of the modern tendency of teams to dispose of their disposable assets, burning through cost-controlled arms the way that man chopped down forests in *The Lorax*. Stuff just isn't built to outlive their original owners anymore.

It's unsurprising, given how well-mined the market for inefficiencies has been of late. The disciples of the early analytics departments, and the disciples of those, have proliferated the league, with only a few backwater holdouts. The league has grown smarter, but every team has learned the same lesson. In fact, the phenomenon creates a peculiar kind of feedback loop: As teams value a specific subset of players or skills, prospective athletes learn to increase their own marketability by conforming themselves to the demands of their prospective employers.

And that's tragic, in the way that the extinction of animals is tragic; a certain amount of biodiversity in baseball has been lost. Shortstops hit like outfielders. Pitchers don't hit at all. Only the catchers remain idiosyncratic, thanks to the defensive demands of their position; eventually they too will be required to produce like everyone else, or they'll meet the fate of their battery mates. A perfect economy requires perfect production.

I mentioned earlier that more and more, I leave thrift stores empty-handed. It is true that I am more discerning than in the past; my bookshelves are full, and there are more streaming films than I will ever be able to watch. But there are other factors at play.

Thrift stores are, in a way, the bond markets of retail. When the economy is rough and other retailers are struggling, more people look secondhand for their products. But as recently as last year, publications were noting a reversal of the trend: Companies like Goodwill and Savers were expanding despite a strong economy. Publications credited a heightened sense of environmentalism and a rejection of cutting-edge fashion as drivers behind the increase, though the more likely answer is the modern American economy hasn't showered its favors equally, particularly among the young.

But it is more than just the economy. Baseball and thrift stores share something else in common, evident in our current conversations about re-starting the sport: They live in the gray area between public service and private enterprise. Thrift stores provide affordable necessities to lower-class citizens, and collectibles and fashion for the middle-class. Because of the success of the latter, prices have gone up across the board. Especially in terms of clothing, the middle-class flight from fashion into vintage has instead carried the aftereffects of fashion, including its costs, into a territory where people just want clothes. But there's another factor in the rise of prices, in the form of the internet.

The Goodwills of the world have grown smarter, too, employing the internet to extract full value from their detritus. Ebay, similarly, has lost much of the charm it had as a new frontier around the turn of the century. Everything has a price point now; even individual taste is no match for the algorithm, because anything rare, no matter how niche its market, is a collectible to someone.

The internet has had the same effect on thrift stores that sabermetrics has had on baseball; its equivalent to OBP was the bar scanner. As detailed in Slate, the rise of second-party stores on eBay and Amazon birthed an entire industry of used-good salespeople, armed with PDAs and scanners, buying books for three dollars to sell online for five. The author, Michael Savitz, reports earning $60,000 by working nearly 80 hours a week; he makes it clear that this is not a vocation of his choosing. It's long hours, with no real creativity or individuality, skimming the cream off of a local establishment and flipping it to someone with a little more money on the other side of the country. And once the vocation exists, the obvious question arises: why wait to put the wares out on the shelves? Why allow value to exist at all?

Nothing is ruined. Thrift stores will continue to sell polo shirts and DVDs, and baseball will continue to exist and make or lose money, depending on who you believe. But as we continue to refine our knowledge, we lose something in the conquest for efficiency, a delight born out of the unknown. The problem isn't the efficiency itself; we can't blame the booksellers, or the people sweeping freeways to collect grams of platinum from damaged catalytic converters. The problem is a system that requires this sort of profit-skimming behavior in order to feed families (or, for corporations, maximize shareholder return).

Tampa Bay Rays 2021

In times like these, with the 2020 season on the brink and the collective bargaining agreement close behind, it can often feel like the current situation is untenable. It can't keep going like this, even if we don't know what to do about it. But as with thrift stores, there's an equally irresistible feeling that it *has* to keep going, that it would be unimaginable to not have this broken, amazing sport. Both industries exist on an invisible foundation of friction, of chaos and unpredictability, even as both see their foundations buffed down to a perfect, untouchable polish. But if COVID-19 and its financial ramifications do, as some have suggested, make it such that the baseball that returns is fundamentally different than the baseball that came before, perhaps this is the time to lean in, and change the game even more. Fix bunting. Make defense more difficult. Create viable, alternate strategies. Add some chaos back into baseball. It's fun when no one knows quite where things are.

—*Patrick Dubuque is an author of Baseball Prospectus.*

Steve Dalkowski Dreaming

by Steven Goldman

We dream of being a pitcher, of starring in the major leagues. Depending on your age and your sense of historical perspective, you might imagine yourself as Walter Johnson, throwing harder than anyone else—hitting more batters than anyone else, too, but always feeling bad about it. You could picture yourself as a Tom Seaver or a David Cone, with all the stuff in the world but still being cerebral about it, thinking about so much more than burning 'em in there. There are so many models one could choose: You could be a Lefty Gomez, Jim Bouton, or Bill Lee, skilled, but not taking the whole thing too seriously, or a Lefty Grove, Bob Gibson, or Steve Carlton, powerful but treating each start like a mission to be survived instead of a game to be enjoyed.

Very few would dream of being Steve Dalkowski, the former Baltimore Orioles prospect who died of COVID-19 last week at the age of 80. Yet, there is something just as noble in Dalkowski's negative accomplishments—and accomplishments is what they are—as there is in the precision-engineered pitching of a Greg Maddux. You have to be very good to be that bad. Dalkowski had all of the stuff of the greatest pitchers but none of the command; his story is not one of failing to conquer his limitations, but striving against one of the cruelest hands that fate or genetics or personality can deal us: A desire to achieve great things which is almost but not quite matched by the ability to meet that goal.

As with Johnson, Grove, Bob Feller, and the rest of the hard-throwing pitchers who played before the advent of modern radar guns, we have to take the word of the players and coaches who saw Dalkowski pitch as to his velocity. He was a hard-drinking, maximum-effort pitcher who, if their memories are to be believed, consistently threw over 100 miles per hour. His was the Maltese Fastball, the stuff that dreams are made of. The problem is that velocity without command and control is still a good distance from utility. Dalkowski was the most effective towel you could design for a fish, the sleekest bathing suit intended to be worn by an astronaut, but that doesn't mean he wasn't beautiful: We can appreciate a journey even if it doesn't end at the intended destination.

Whether because of sloppy mechanics he couldn't calm, an inability to understand that a consistent 98 in the strike zone would likely be more effective than a consistent 110 out of it, or all that beer, Dalkowski could never make the adjustments that pitchers like Feller and Nolan Ryan made before him, possibly because he had so far to go: Feller, who never pitched in the minors, came up at 17 and spent three years walking almost seven batters per nine innings before settling in at 3.8 beginning when he was 20. Ryan started out walking over six batters per nine but gradually improved as his long career played out; for him to go from 6.2 walks per nine with the 1966 Greenville Mets to 3.7 with the 1989 Texas Rangers represents a 40 percent reduction. An equivalent improvement by Dalkowski would still have left him walking over 11 batters per nine innings.

Dalkowski was like *The Room* of pitchers, a player so bad he became good again. Cal Ripken, Sr., who both played with and managed Dalkowski, recalled in a 1979 *Sporting News* "where are they now" piece the occasion when the pitcher crossed up his catcher and his fastball, "hit the plate umpire smack in the mask. The mask broke all to pieces and the umpire wound up in the hospital for three days with a concussion. If they ever had a radar gun in those days, I'll bet Dalkowski would have been timed at 110 miles an hour."

Signed by the Orioles out of New Britain High in Connecticut in 1957, Dalkowski was sent to Kingsport in the Appalachian League, where he pitched 62 innings. He allowed only 22 hits in 62 innings, or 3.2 per nine, a number with no equivalent in major league history (though Aroldis Chapman came close in 2014), and also struck out 121 (17.6 per nine) and walked 129 (18.7). He was also charged with 39 wild pitches. That June, one of his fastballs clipped a Dodgers prospect named Bob Beavers and carried away part of his ear. "The first pitch was over the backstop, the second pitch was called a strike, I didn't think it was," Beavers said last year. "The third pitch hit me and knocked me out, so I don't remember much after that. I couldn't get in the sun for a while, and I never did play baseball again." Former minor leaguer Ron Shelton based the *Bull Durham* pitcher Nuke LaLoosh on Dalkowski. And yet, to see him as a figure of fun, an amusing loser, is to misunderstand something unique and strange.

Dalkowski kept on posting some of the strangest lines in baseball history. Pitching for the Stockton Ports of the Class C California League in 1960, he struck out 262 and walked 262 in 170 innings. Yet, he did improve, especially after pitching for Earl Weaver at Elmira in 1962. Weaver had previously had Dalkowski at Aberdeen in 1959, but wasn't ready to grapple with him then. This time he was. "I had grown more and more concerned about players with great physical abilities who could not learn to correct certain basic deficiencies no matter how much you instructed or drilled them," he related in his autobiography, *It's What You Learn After You Know It All That Counts*. He got permission from the Orioles to give all of his players the Stanford-Binet IQ test. "Dalkowski finished in the 1 percentile in his ability to understand facts. Steve, it was said to say, had the ability to do everything but learn." [sic]

IQ tests are problematic diagnostic tools, so take Weaver's estimate of Dalkowski's mental capabilities with a grain of salt. What's important is that even if he got to the right answer by way of the wrong reason, Weaver had learned something valuable. His insight was to stop asking Dalkowski to learn new pitches and just let him get by with the two that he had. Were Dalkowski a prospect today, that would have been a no-brainer: Can't develop a third pitch? The bullpen is right over there, sir. Player development wasn't like that then, but Weaver, temporarily Dalkowski's mentor, could let him work with what he had. According to Weaver, the pitcher responded: "In the final 57 innings he pitched that season Dalkowski gave up 1 earned run, struck out 110 batters, and walked only 11." It's not true—as per the *Elmira Star-Gazette*, as of late July, Dalkowski had walked 71 in 106 innings and finished with 114 in 160 innings, which means Dalkowski's control actually faded at the end of the season rather than improved—but that doesn't mean it didn't happen in some sense, just that it didn't happen that way. Again, it's the journey, not the destination, and his ERA was 3.04 so *something* had gone right.

Also along the way: The next spring, Orioles manager Billy Hitchcock was rooting for Dalkowski to make the team as a long-man—maybe Weaver had gotten through to him. There were things out of Weaver's control, like the universe's twisted sense of humor: that March, Dalkowski's elbow went "twang."

You sometimes read that it was the Orioles' insistence on Dalkowski learning the curve that did him in, but even if they hadn't learned their lesson, the injury was probably just a coincidence: Dalkowski had thrown an incredible number of pitches over the previous few years. Still, it testifies to the dangers of trying to get what you want and risking the loss of what you had. Dalkowski tried to come back, but the 110-mph stuff was gone. A pitcher with no control and no stuff is...a civilian. What followed were years of vagabond living, arrests for drunkenness. There were Alcoholics Anonymous meetings, assistance from baseball alumni associations, but none of it took. From the 1990s until the time of his passing he dwelt in an assisted living facility, suffering from alcohol-related dementia. He'd been a heavy drinker since his teenage years. As with all those pitches per game, there was a price to be paid. You make choices on the journey and some of them are irrevocable. It's like a fairy tale: "Bite of poison apple? Don't mind if I do."

In the aforementioned *Sporting News* profile, Chuck Stevens, the head of the Association of Professional Ballplayers of America, a ballplayer charity, said, "I've got nothing against drinking. I do it myself sometimes. But, I don't condone common drunkenness. We went through lots of heartache and many dollars, but Dalkowski didn't want to help himself and we weren't going to keep him drunk." The journey is *un*like a fairy tale: No one will come along and kiss it better, not if they're busy forming judgments.

In the end, we are left with a sort of philosophical chicken/egg conundrum: Is failing to meet your goals evidence of unfulfilled potential or the lack of it? Isn't what you did by definition what you were capable of doing? Or could you have broken through to something better with the right help, the right lucky break? These are unanswerable questions, and how we try to answer them may say more about us than about the people we're judging.

No pitcher ever has it easy. *All* pitchers must work hard. *All* pitchers must refine their craft. It's almost never just about *stuff*. Dalkowski dreaming is no insult to the great pitchers who made it; from Pete Alexander to Max Scherzer, they have all earned their way up. And yet, if it is true that we can only do as much as we can do, then the journey would be more of an adventure, the ultimate triumph or defeat more noble, if like Dalkowski we lacked 100 percent of the confidence, the command, the self-possession, the commitment, the resistance to making bad decisions that so many great players possess—to be gloriously human. Or, to put it more succinctly, it would be fun to be able to throw as hard as any person ever has. Even if just for a moment, and even if nothing more came of it than that, no one could say you hadn't lived life to the fullest.

—*Steven Goldman is an author of Baseball Prospectus.*

A Reward For A Functioning Society

by Cory Frontin and Craig Goldstein

On July 5, Nationals reliever Sean Doolittle said in the middle of a press conference regarding the restart of Major League Baseball and what would later be known as summer camp, "sports are like the reward of a functioning society." This sentence was amidst a much longer, thoughtful reply about the societal and health conditions under which MLB players were being brought back. It's a very similar sentiment to one Jane McManus used on April 7, when she discussed the White House's meeting with sports commissioners. She said "sports are the effect of a functioning society—not the precursor."

Both versions of the same sentiment spoke to a laudable ideal in the context of a country that was not addressing a rampaging virus, and opting instead to bring sports back for the feeling of normalcy rather than the reality of it. "Priorities," as McManus said.

On Wednesday, the NBA's Milwaukee Bucks conducted a wildcat/political strike, refusing to come out for Game 5 of their playoff series against the Orlando Magic. The Magic refused to accept the forfeit, and shortly thereafter other playoff series were threatened by player strikes. Eventually the league moved to postpone that day's games, folding to players leveraging their united power.

The backdrop against which these actions took place was the shooting by police of Jacob Blake. Blake was shot in the back seven times by police, as he attempted to get into his vehicle. He managed to survive the assault, but is paralyzed from the waist down.

⚾   ⚾   ⚾

The step taken to walk out, first by the Milwaukee Bucks, then subsequently by other NBA, WNBA, and MLB teams, was a step toward upholding the virtue of the sentiment described by McManus and Doolittle. But that sentiment does not align with the broad history of sports in this and other countries, a history that contradicts the core of the idealistic statement.

Sports have been a significant part of American society for most of its existence, expanding in importance and influence in recent years. The idea that society was functioning in a way that was worthy of the reward of sports for most of that time is laughable. Much of America is not functioning and has not functioned for Black people, full stop. The oppressed people at the center of this political act by players, specifically Black players, in concert throughout the NBA and in fits and starts throughout Major League Baseball, have not known a society that functions for them rather than *because* of them.

Politics has been part of the sports landscape since the inception of sport, but for just about as long people have bemoaned its presence. Sports are to be an escape, it is said. An escape from what, though? A functioning society?

No, the presence of sports has never signified a cultural or political system that is on the up and up. Rather, the presence of sports *reflect and reinforce the society that produces them*.

⚾ ⚾ ⚾

The Negro Leagues were born out of societal dysfunction. The need for entirely separate leagues, composed of Black and Latino players barred from the Major Leagues because of racism? That is not a functioning society, and yet there were sports.

Even the integration of players from the Negro Leagues resulted in a transfer of power and wealth from Black-owned businesses and communities and into white ones, mirroring the dysfunction that had bled into every aspect of American society at the time. Japheth Knopp noted in the Spring 2016 Baseball Research Journal:

> *The manner in which integration in baseball—and in American businesses generally—occurred was not the only model which was possible. It was likely not even the best approach available, but rather served the needs of those in already privileged positions who were able to control not only the manner in which desegregation occurred, but the public perception of it as well in order to exploit the situation for financial gain. Indeed, the very word integration may not be the most applicable in this context because what actually transpired was not so much the fair and equitable combination of two subcultures into one equal and more homogenous group, but rather the reluctant allowance—under certain preconditions—for African Americans to be assimilated into white society.*

To understand the value of a movement, though, is not to understand how it is co-opted by ownership, but to know the people it brings together and what they demand. When Jackie Robinson—the player who demarcated the inevitability of the end of the Negro leagues—attended the March on Washington for Jobs and Freedom in 1963, he did so with his family and marched alongside the people. He stood alongside hundreds of thousands to fight for their common civil and labor rights. "The moral arc of the universe is long," many freedom fighters have echoed, "but it bends towards justice." The bend, it is less frequently said, happens when a great mass of people place the moral arc of the universe on their knee and apply force, as Jackie, his family, and thousands of others did that day.

⚾ ⚾ ⚾

Of course, taking the moral arc of the universe down from the mantle and bending it is not without risk. Perhaps the outsized influence of athletes is itself a mark of a dysfunctional society, but, nonetheless, hundreds of athletes woke up on Wednesday morning with the power to bring in millions of dollars in revenues. That very power, as we would come to find out, was matched with the equal and opposite power to *not* bring those revenues. That power, in hands ranging from the Milwaukee Bucks, to Kenny Smith in the *Inside the NBA* Studio, from the unexpected ally, Josh Hader, and his largely white teammates to the notably Black Seattle Mariners, would be exercised for a single demand: the end to state violence against Black people. Not unlike the March itself, it sat at the intersection of the civil rights of Black Americans and bold labor action. The March on Washington stood in the face of a false notion of integration—against an integration of extraction but not one of equality—and proposed something different. Just the same, the acts of solidarity of August 26, 2020 will be remembered in stark defiance of MLB's BLM-branded, but ultimately empty displays on opening weekend.

Bold defiance like this can never be without risk. By choosing to exercise this power, the Milwaukee Bucks took a risk. They risked vitriol and backlash from those they disagreed with. They risked fines or seeing their contracts voided, as a walkout like this is prohibited by their CBA. They risked forfeiting a playoff game, one that, as the No. 1 seed in the playoffs, they'd worked all year to attain. They didn't know how Orlando would respond. It wasn't clear that other teams throughout the league would follow suit in solidarity. And it wasn't known the league would accept these actions and moderately co-opt them by "postponing" games that would have featured no players.

If the league reschedules the games, some of the athletes' risk—their shared sacrifice—will be diminished, in retrospect. But they did not know any of that when they took that risk. And it is often left to athletes to take these risks when others in society won't, especially those of their same socioeconomic status and levels of influence.

It is athletes, specifically BIPOC athletes, that take them, though, because they live with the risk of being something other than white in this country every day. They are no strangers to the realities of police brutality. It seems incongruous then, to say that sports are a reward for a functioning society when we rely on athletes to lead us closer to being a functioning society. Luckily, our beloved athletes, WNBA players first and foremost among them, understand what sports truly are: a pipebender for the moral arc of the universe.

> *—Craig Goldstein is editor in chief of Baseball Prospectus. Cory Frontin is an author of Baseball Prospectus.*

Index of Names

Adames, Willy 16
Anderson, Nick 42
Archer, Chris 80
Arozarena, Randy 18, 90
Baz, Shane 81, 90
Beeks, Jalen 44
Bitsko, Nick 81, 97
Brosseau, Mike 20
Brujan, Vidal 74, 92
Castillo, Diego 46
Catalina, Neraldo 99
Chirinos, Yonny 48
Choi, Ji-Man 22
Curtiss, John 50
Díaz, Yandy 24
Drake, Oliver 52
Edwards, Xavier 75, 94
Fairbanks, Pete 54
Fleming, Josh 56, 99
Franco, Wander 76, 89
Glasnow, Tyler 58
Hernandez, Heriberto 77, 98
Hernandez, Ronaldo 77, 97
Honeywell, Brent 82, 98
Hulsizer, Niko 100
Hunt, Blake 96
Johnson, Seth 98
Jones, Greg 95
Kiermaier, Kevin 26
Kittredge, Andrew 82
Lowe, Brandon 28
Lowe, Josh 78, 96
Margot, Manuel 30
Martinez, Pedro 98
McClanahan, Shane 83, 93
McKay, Brendan 84, 96
Meadows, Austin 32
Mejía, Francisco 78
Padlo, Kevin 99
Patino, Luis 60, 91
Phillips, Brett 34
Plassmeyer, Michael 100
Poche, Colin 85
Reed, Cody 62
Richards, Trevor 64
Roe, Chaz 86
Ryan, Joe 86, 97
Sherriff, Will 66
Strotman, Drew 97
Thompson, Ryan 68
Tsutsugo, Yoshi 36
Wacha, Michael 70
Walls, Taylor 100
Wendle, Joey 38
Wilcox, Cole 87, 94
Williams, Alika 99
Yarbrough, Ryan 72
Zunino, Mike 40

For the Joy of Keeping Score

THIRTY81 Project is an ongoing graphic design project focused on the ballparks of baseball. Since being established in 2013, scorecards have been a fundemantal part of the effort. Each two-page card is uniquely ballpark-centric — there are 30 variants — and designed with both beginning and veteran scorekeepers in mind. Evolving over the years with suggestions from fans, broadcasters, and official scorers, the sheets are freely available to everyone as printable letter-size PDFs at the project webshop: www.THIRTY81Project.com

Download, Print, Score, Repeat ...

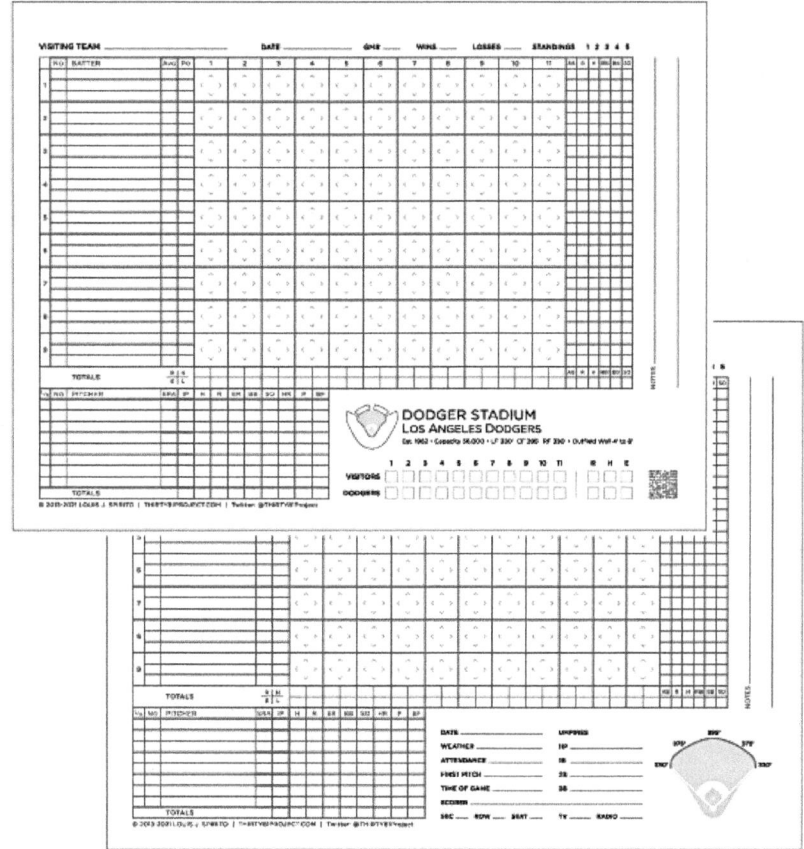